CHRIS SCARRE

THE PENGUIN
HISTORICAL ATLAS
OF ANCIENT ROME

PENGUIN BOOKS

Published by the Penguin Group
Penguin Books Ltd, 27 Wrights Lane, London W8 5TZ, England
Penguin Putnam Inc., 375 Hudson Street, New York, New York 10014, USA
Penguin Books Australia Ltd, Ringwood, Victoria, Australia
Penguin Books Canada Ltd, 10 Alcorn Avenue, Toronto, Ontario, Canada M4V 3B2
Penguin Books (NZ) Ltd, Private Bag 102902, NSMC, Auckland, New Zealand

Penguin Books Ltd, Registered Offices: Harmondsworth, Middlesex, England

First published simultaneously by Viking and Penguin Books 1995
7 9 10 8 6

Printed and bound in Great Britain by The Bath Press, Avon

Foreword

Roman civilization is one of the great unifying factors in the history of Europe and the Mediterranean. The extensive empire ruled by the Romans stretched from the sands of the Sahara to the mouth of the Rhine, and from the Atlantic in the west to the Euphrates in the east. It has left us its legacy in the form of Roman law, which still underlies many western-inspired legal systems, and in the Romance languages—French, Spanish, Portuguese, Italian and Romanian—derived from Latin, which are still spoken not only in former Roman territories but in countries of the New World as well as the Old. Furthermore, Roman cities lie beneath many of our modern centres, and the state religion of the late Roman world—Christianity—remains the dominant faith throughout most of Europe today.

The Penguin Historical Atlas of Ancient Rome is an introduction to the Roman Empire based on maps. The Romans themselves made maps of their empire, though little of these have survived apart from the so-called Peutinger Table (a medieval copy) and fragments such as the marble map of Rome. It is other sources, then, which have been used to compile the present volume, and they are of broadly two kinds: historical and literary on the one hand (what the Romans said about themselves), and archaeological and architectural on the other.

Each of these sources has its own particular role. The details of historical events themselves are known to us mainly through written texts in Latin or Greek. These include works of famous historians such as Livy and Tactius, and social or official documents such as letters and laws. Coins and inscriptions provide abundant further evidence, and can often be dated precisely. Archaeology, on the other hand, can sometimes be tied into the history but essentially tells us a different kind of story. We may remember the Romans in terms of kings and consuls, battles and emperors, but for the majority of Roman inhabitants, those who ploughed the fields and tended the olive groves, by far the best testimony comes from archaeological remains of ordinary houses, farms and workshops. No one source of evidence, however, is intrinsically better then the others; it is by using them together that we gain the fullest insight into the world of ancient Rome.

Chris Scarre,
Cambridge, 1995

Contents

Timeline: 800–85 BC

THE ROMAN STATE	BUILDING & CONSTRUCTION	LITERATURE & PHILOSOPHY	ASIA, AFRICA & THE MEDITERRANEAN
BC			
			814 (trad) Carthage founded
c. 800–750 Iron-Age settlement on Palatine Hill			
753 (trad) Romulus founds Rome			c. 750 Greek colonies in Sicily and S. Italy
642–17 Roman power extends to coast			
c. 616–510 Rome under Etruscan dominance	c. 600 Forum laid out as public square		c. 600 Greek colony at Massilia (Marseille)
			c. 550 Persian empire of Cyrus
534–510 Rome controls 350 sq m of territory			525 Persian king Cambyses conquers Egypt
510 Republic established under 2 annually-elected consuls	510 (trad) Temple of Jupiter on the Capitol		
	484 Temple of Castor dedicated	486 death of Buddha	
		479 death of Confucius	480 Greeks defeat Persians at Salamis
451–50 Decemvirate—council of 10 assume magistrates' powers			447 Parthenon begun
			431–404 Peloponnesian War between Sparta and Athens
396 Romans capture Etruscan city of Veii		399 death of Socrates	
390 Celts sack Rome			
	378 Servian Wall round Rome	c. 380 Plato (427–347) founds Academy at Athens	
356 first plebeian dictator, G. Marcus Rutilus			353 Mausoleum of Halicarnassus
343–1 First Samnite War	344 Temple of Juno Moneta		343 last native pharaoh of Egypt ousted by Persians
340–38 Latin War: Rome wins control of Latium			333–323 Alexander the Great conquers Persian Empire
327–04 Second Samnite War			Hellenistic monarchies established from partition of Alexander's empire: Ptolemaic kingdom in Egypt (304), Seleucid empire in Syria & Middle East
298–90 Third Samnite War. Roman territory extends from Bay of Naples to the Adriatic	312 Via Appia, Aqua Appia built under censor Appius Claudius	290 Library of Alexandria founded	
281–275 Romans repel invasion by Pyrrhus, king of Epirus	281 Via Appia extended to Tarentum		272–32 Mauryan Emperor Ashoka promotes Buddhism in S. Asia
246–241 First Punic War gives Rome control of Sicily			240 Bactria & Parthia secede from Seleucid empire
		Plautus (c. 254–184): comedies	237–218 Carthaginians conquer southern Spain
218–201 Second Punic War: Romans repel Hannibal's invasion of Italy and conquer much of Spain		Ennius (239–169): plays, annals	221–206 Qin dynasty unites China as single state
			206 death of Shih-huang-ti, first emperor of China
202–191 Romans conquer Cisalpine Gaul		Polybius (c. 203–120): Histories (Gk)	202 China reunited by Han dynasty
190 Romans defeat Antiochus the Great at Magnesia		Terence (c. 190–159): comedies	
	174 Circus Maximus rebuilt		170 expansion of Graeco-Bactrian kingdom under Demetrius & Eucratides
		161 Greek philosophers expelled from Rome	156–87 Wu–ti greatest emperor of Chinese Han dynasty
149–6 Third Punic War: Romans destroy Carthage; Africa a Roman province.		149 Cato's Origins published	
146 Mummius sacks Corinth; Greece a Roman province (Achaea)	146 Temple of Jupiter Stator, first marble temple at Rome		
	144 Aqua Marcia		141 Parthians conquer Mesopotamia
135–2 slave uprising in Sicily	142 Pons Aemilius		
133 reforms of tribune Tiberius Gracchus lead to his murder			130 Graeco-Bactrian kingdom falls to Kushans
123–2 tribune Gaius Gracchus murdered after attempting reform	121 Via Domitia		
107–100 Marius dominant in Rome			112 Mithridates becomes king of Pontus and conquers Crimea
102 Marius defeats Teutones and (101) Cimbri			106 first caravan trade between Parthia & China
91–89 Social War: Rome defeats rebellious Italian allies, but grants major concessions			

84 BC–99 AD

THE ROMAN STATE	BUILDING & CONSTRUCTION	LITERATURE & PHILOSOPHY	ASIA & AFRICA
83–79 civil war: Sulla becomes dictator and purges opponents	*c.* 80 Temple of Fortuna at Praeneste 78 Tabularium at Rome		
73–71 Spartacus leads slave uprising in Capua		Lucretius (*c.* 99–55): philosophical poem *The Nature of Things*	
64 Pompey conquers Syria 63 Romans annexe Judaea 60 First Triumvirate: Pompey, Caesar, Crassus 58–51 Caesar conquers Gaul 53 Crassus defeated and killed by Parthians at Carrhae	62 Pons Fabricius 55 Theatre of Pompey	Catullus (*c.* 84–54): poems and epigrams Julius Caesar (100–44): *Gallic Wars; Civil Wars*	55 Hermaus, last Indo-Bactrian king, defeated by Scythians 51 Ptolemy XXII and Cleopatra rulers of Egypt
48 Caesar defeats Pompey at Pharsalus. Pompey flees to Egypt and is killed 45 Caesar defeats Pompeians at Munda 44 Caesar dicatator for life; assassinated by Brutus & Cassius 43 Cicero killed. Second Triumvirate— Antony, Octavian & Lepidus—cemented by marriage of Antony to Octavian's sister Octavia 42 Brutus and Cassius defeated at Philippi	46 Forum of Julius Caesar	46 Julius Caesar reforms calendar Sallust (86–35 BC), historian: *Jugurthine War, Catiline Conspiracy* Varro (116–27 BC): *On Rural Life*	37 Parthians invade Syria
37 Antony marries Cleopatra at Antioch 31 Octavian & Agrippa defeat Antony & Cleopatra at naval battle of Actium 30 Antony & Cleopatra commit suicide. Octavian sole ruler of Roman world. Egypt a Roman province 27 Octavian assumes title Augustus	28 Carthage refounded as Roman colony 28 Mausoleum of Augustus 27 Pantheon of Marcus Agrippa 13 Theatre of Marcellus 9 Ara Pacis Augustae 2 Forum of Augustus	Virgil (70–19): *Georgics, Eclogues;* epic poem *Aeneid* links founding of Rome to Homer's Troy Strabo (64 BC–AD 21) writes his *Geography* at Alexandria Horace (65–8): *Odes, Carmen Saeculare* Livy (59 BC–AD 17) writes "official" history of Rome	25 Aelius Gallus leads expedition to Marib (Yemen) 19 Herod rebuilds Temple at Jerusalem
12–9 Romans conquer Germany as far as the Elbe			
AD			
6 planned conquest of central Europe abandoned after rebellion in Balkans 9 three legions under Varus wiped out by Germans. Roman frontier pulled back to Rhine		Ovid (43 BC–AD 18): *The Art of Love, Metamorphoses.* Banished to Black Sea coast by Augustus, AD 8	9 Wang-Mang deposes Han dynasty in China
14 Augustus dies, succeeded by his stepson Tiberius 17 Cappadocia & Commagene an imperial province	14 Pont du Gard aqueduct near Nimes 15 Samian ware potteries founded in Gaul		
	21-22 Castra Praetoria		25 Han dynasty restored
27 Tiberius retires to Capri			29 Jesus Christ crucified
37 Tiberius dies; Gaius (Caligula) succeeds 41 Caligula assassinated; Claudius emperor 42 Mauretania annexed 43 invasion of Britain. Lycia an imperial province 54 Claudius dies; Nero emperor 60 revolt of Iceni in Britain; crushed in 61 64 fire and persecution of Christians in Rome 66 Jewish revolt 68–9 revolt of Vindex & suicide of Nero. Civil war. Vespasian emperor 70 Sack of Jerusalem	64 Nero's "Golden House"	Hero of Alexandria (fl. 50) invents rudimentary steam turbine Seneca (d. 65): tragedies & philosophy Lucan (39–65): heroic poem *Pharsalia.* Petronius (d. 66): comic novel *Satyricon.* All three writers forced to commit suicide by Nero Flavius Josephus (34–*c.* 98): *History of the Jewish War; Jewish Antiquities* Pliny the Elder (23–79): *Natural History.* Dies observing eruption of Vesuvius	60 Nero sends expedition to explore Meroe (Sudan)
79 eruption of Vesuvius destroys Pompeii & Herculaneum	80 Colosseum, Arch of Titus, Domus Flavia on Palatine		91 Chinese defeat Hsiung-nu (Huns) in Mongolia
96 Emperor Domitian assassinated; Nerva emperor 97 Nerva adopts Trajan 98 Trajan emperor		Martial (40–104): *Epigrams* Tacitus (*c.* 55–*c.* 117): *Annals; Histories; Agricola; Germania*	97 Chinese ambassador Kan Ying visits Antioch

Timeline: 100–363 AD

THE ROMAN STATE	BUILDING & CONSTRUCTION	LITERATURE & PHILOSOPHY	ASIA & AFRICA
101–2 First Dacian War 105–6 Second Dacian War; Dacia a Roman province 106 Arabia annexed	100 Roman colony of Timgad founded	Pliny the Younger (61–113): *Panegyric of Trajan;* 10 vols of letters	105 paper invented in China
113–7 Parthian War: Armenia & N. Mesopotamia annexed. Trajan dies. Hadrian succeeds & halts policy of expansion	112 Trajan's Forum & Column	Plutarch (c. 45–125): *Parallel Lives* (Gk) of Greeks and Romans	120 Roman merchant Maes explores Central Asia & Silk Route
122 Hadrian strengthens Rhine-Danube frontier	118 Pantheon rebuilt 122 Hadrian's Wall 124 Hadrian's Library & Arch at Athens	Juvenal (60–c. 130): *Satires* Claudius Ptolemy (fl. 125–148) compiles his *Geography* at Alexandria	
130 founding of Aelia Capitolina on site of Jerusalem sparks Jewish revolt		Suetonius (c. 75– c. 160): *Lives of the Caesars; Illustrious Men*	
138 Hadrian dies, succeeded by Antoninus Pius	138 completion of Zaghouan aqueduct to supply Carthage		
161 Marcus Aurelius & Lucius Verus joint emperors 165 Romans capture Dura Europus, sack Parthian capital Ctesiphon. 167 Quadi & Marcomanni invade Italy & besiege Aquileia 168–75 wars against Quadi & Marcomanni		Apuleius (c. 125–?): *The Golden Ass* anonymous poem *Pervigilium Veneris* (The Vigil of Venus)	166 embassy from Marcus Aurelius reaches China
192/3 assassination of Commodus leads to civil war in which Severus becomes emperor 198 Severus captures Nisibis and sacks Ctesiphon. N. Mesopotamia a Roman province 209–11 Severus campaigns in Scotland. Dies at York 212 Caracalla extends citizenship to all free inhabitants of empire	193–211 Severan wing of Palatine palace, Septizonium, Arch of Severus	Marcus Aurelius (121-180): *Meditations* (Gk) Tertullian (c. 150–230): *Apologia; The Blood of Christ* Cassius Dio (c. 155–230): *Roman History* (Gk)	
217 Caracalla murdered	216 Baths of Caracalla		
230 Persians invade Mesopotamia 237–8 Persians attack Mesopotamia		*Antonine Itinerary* lists routes and mileages throughout Roman Empire	220 fall of Han dynasty in China 226 Parthian rulers of Iran overthrown by Persian Sassanian dynasty
250 Emperor Decius persecutes Christians 251 Decius killed in battle against Goths 253 Persians capture Antioch 254 Marcomanni attack Ravenna. 256 Gothic fleet attacks Asia Minor, Franks attack lower Rhine			Persian holy man Mani (216–77) founds Manichaeism 252 first Persian invasion of Syria
260 Emperor Valerian captured by Persians. Breakaway empire in Gaul 262 Agri Decumates abandoned 268 Gallienus defeats Goths at Naissus but is assassinated soon after 270 Aurelian emperor. Dacia abandoned 273 Aurelian recaptures Gallic & Palmyrene empires 282 Carus invades Persia	271 Aurelian Wall around Rome	Plotinus (205–69), neo-Platonist philosopher influential at Rome 269 St Antony becomes a hermit, founding eastern monasticism	259 second Persian invasion of Syria
293 Diocletian establishes tetrarchy			
303-5 "Great persecution" of Christians 305 Diocletian & Maximian abdicate 313 freedom of worship restored to Christians			304 Hsiung-nu (Huns) invade China
324 Constantine sole ruler 325 Council of Nicaea 330 Constantinople becomes capital of empire 337 death of Constantine; empire shared between his 3 sons	c. 315 Basilica Nova completed 329 St Peter's, Rome, completed 324–337 Great Palace, Constantinople, churches of Holy Apostles & St Eirene, Constantinople 360 first church of St Sophia, Constantinople, completed		
356–60 Julian fights Franks & Alemanni in Gaul			
363 Emperor Julian killed fighting Persians			

364–540 AD

WESTERN EMPIRE	EASTERN EMPIRE	BUILDING & CONSTRUCTION	LITERATURE & PHILOSOPHY	ASIA & AFRICA
364 empire divided between brothers Valentinian (west) and Valens (east)		375 Aqueduct of Valens, Constantinople	Zosismus: *New History* (Gk) Ammianus Marcellinus (*c.* 330–*c.* 393), last great Roman historian *Augustan History* compiled Eunapius (345–420): *Lives of the Sophists* (Gk)	375 Huns defeat Goths on R. Dnieper; they flee towards Danube & Roman territory
	378 Valens defeated and killed by Goths at battle of Adrianople			379 Buddhism becomes state religion in China
	391 Theodosius outlaws paganism 396 Visigoths pillage Greece		*c.* 400 *Notitia Dignitatum* lists civil and military posts throughout empire	
401–2 Stilicho repels Visigoth invasion of Italy. Imperial court moves from Milan to Ravenna			Claudian (d. 404): poems	
406 Vandals, Alans & Suebi cross Rhine & ravage Gaul			St Augustine of Hippo (354–430): *Confessions; City of God*	
408 Stilicho executed on treason charge	408 Arcadius dies. Theodosius II emperor in East			
410 Visigoths sack Rome. Emperor Honorius tells Britons to defend themselves		413 Theodosian Walls, Constantinople 424 Mausoleum of Galla Placidia at Ravenna		
418 Visigoths establish capital at Toulouse *c.* 425–500 Angles, Saxons & Jutes settle in Britain	421–2 East Romans defeat Persians			
429–39 Vandals conquer North Africa	441–3 East Romans defeat Persians, but are defeated by Huns in Balkans		438 Theodosian Code 431–89 Sidonius Apollinaris, Gallo-Roman writer	
451 Aëtius repels Huns	451 Council of Chalcedon			
455 Vandals under Gaiseric sack Rome				
476 last western emperor deposed. Odoacer king at Rome	475–7 Emperor Zeno temporarily deposed by usurper Basiliscus			484 Shah Firuz, Persian king, killed by Huns
482 Clovis king of Franks	481 Zeno makes Ostrogoth Theodoric a consul 488 Zeno sends Theodoric to rule Italy	480 Church of Qa'lat Si'mon (Simon Stylites), Syria		
493 Theodoric king at Rome	491 Anastasius becomes emperor in East			
507 Franks drive Visigoths from Gaul into Spain		526 Mausoleum of Theodoric at Ravenna	Boëthius (*c.* 470–525): *The Consolation of Philosophy*	
511 Clovis dies; Frankish kingdom divided				
	527 Justinian becomes emperor in East			
529 Benedict of Nursia founds Benedictine order at Monte Cassino		532 Justinian begins rebuilding of Haghia Sophia at Constantinople	528–9 Justinian's *Code of Civil Laws* Cassiodorus (*c.* 490–583): *Variae* (letters)	
540 Byzantine reconquest of Italy				

I: From City to Empire

The city of Rome began life as a modest village in the region of Italy known as Latium. Nobody could have predicted that this undistinguished settlement—merely one of several local centres gradually developing into cities during the 7th and 6th centuries BC—would eventually become mistress not only of all Italy, but of the entire Mediterranean world.

Our knowledge of early Rome is based on two sources of evidence: the traditional histories written by Livy and others several centuries later; and the findings of archaeology. Legend held that the Romans traced their ancestry back to Aeneas, the hero who escaped from the sack of Troy carrying his father Anchises on his back. His subsequent travels took him to Carthage, where he met and fell in love with Dido before forsaking her and settling in Latium. There his son founded the city of Alba Longa, and it was from the kings of Alba Longa that Romulus and Remus, the founders of Rome, were directly descended.

Above: the Etruscans were accomplished bronze-workers, producing distinctive and powerful sculptures. This bronze chimaera—a mythical creature—was found near Arezzo and dates from the 4th century BC.

Much of this is evident invention. Troy, we now know, was sacked in the 12th or 13th century BC, whereas Carthage was only founded in the 8th or 9th. The idea that Trojan refugees sought refuge in central Italy is probably also pure fiction. But the story of Romulus and Remus founding the city of Rome may incorpororate elements of truth. For it was in the 8th century that two existing settlements, one on the Palatine Hill, the other on the Quirinal, coalesced to form a single village. This corresponds in time approximately with the traditional foundation of Rome by Romulus in 753 BC. Early Rome has been given especially vivid form by the discovery early this century of oval hut foundations on the Palatine Hill, and by burials (both inhumations and cremations with "hut-urns") in the Forum valley and on the Esquiline Hill. Some of these burials date back as far as the 10th century BC, long before Romulus's supposed foundation.

Right: the most impressive of Etruscan sites today is the Banditaccia cemetery at Cerveteri. Founded in the 7th century BC, this vast necropolis is dominated by a series of large circular tombs, mostly rock-cut, capped by domed mounds. Around and among them are clusters of less grandiose burial places, including "streets" of rectangular tombs.

Above: *it was the Etruscans who constructed the first major roads and bridges in central Italy. The road leading north from the Etruscan city of Vulci crossed the deep, narrow valley of the river Fiora on the Ponte della Badia. The original bridge consisted of stone piers supporting a wooden superstructure, but the latter was replaced by stone arches in around the 1st century BC.*

The nascent settlement of Rome soon found itself at war with its powerful neighbours, the Sabines. According to tradition, Romulus enticed the Sabines to a feast, during which the Romans seized the Sabine women as their wives. This, again, is probably legend which incorporates a germ of truth, since Sabine influence was strong in early Rome and the eventual compromise, by which Rome was ruled alternately by Roman and Sabine kings, may reflect Rome's origin in the coalescence of two ethnically different communities.

From Village to City

The four earliest kings were shadowy characters, village leaders rather than powerful monarchs, and the settlement itself was small and undistinguished. Major change began to take place during the 7th century, when tiled roofs and stone foundations appear, culminating in the draining of the Forum area and its laying out as a public square: a formal city centre. This coincided with the appearance of new rulers, the Etruscans.

According to legend the first Etruscan ruler, Tarquinius Priscus, took control of Rome by peaceful means, gaining the acquiescence and support of the leading families. He may well have had much to offer the early Romans, since the Etruscans had a flourishing network of city-states in the region to the north of Rome, and Rome stood at a crucial bridging point on the Tiber which gave the Etruscans access to Latium and beyond. Rome never became an Etruscan city-state in the strict sense of the term, but it took on many Etruscan trappings. It was especially important to the Etruscans since the latter had established a major zone of influence in Campania to the south, and the Tiber bridge was the strategic artery of communication between the homeland and these southern outposts.

The Etruscans gave Rome writing (an alphabet they in turn had taken from the Greeks), public buildings (including the Temple of Jupiter on the Capitol) and a new political, social and military organisation. The traditional symbols of power, the *fasces* (bundles of rods and axes, which have given their name to fascism) were also Etruscan in origin. Under the Etruscan kings, Rome became the undisputed leader of a large section of Latium extending from the Alban Hills in the east to the Tiber mouth in the west. The Romans retained their own language, however, though Etruscan families took up residence in the city, and a number of Etruscan inscriptions have been found there. Yet it was not without difficulty that the Romans eventually freed themselves from Etruscan overlordship.

The Birth of the Republic

The Etruscans ruled Rome for a little over a century; the traditional dates are 616 BC for the accession of the first Etruscan king, Tarquinius Priscus, and 510 BC for the expulsion of the last, Tarquinius Superbus—"the proud". (Between them came a Latin king, Servius Tullius, son-in-law of Tarquinius Priscus.) Livy tells us it was the rape of Lucretia by Sextus, son of Tarquin the Proud, which incited rebellion by a group of Roman aristocrats led by Lucius Junius Brutus. The Tarquins were expelled from Rome, and a new constitution devised, whereby power rested in the hands of the senate (the assembly of leading citizens), who delegated executive action to a pair of consuls who were elected from among their number to serve for one year. Thus was born the Roman Republic.

In reality, the story was less simple, for the Etruscans did not so easily relinquish control of their crucial Tiber bridgehead. Tarquin the Proud sought help from Lars Porsenna, ruler of the Etruscan city of Clusium. According to Livy, the Romans beat off this attack, notably by Horatius's heroic stand at the Tiber bridge. Most likely, however, Porsenna did recapture Rome, but failed to hold it for long. The Latin cities banded together with Rome to throw off the Etruscan yoke, and won a major victory at Aricia in 506 BC. Henceforth, though Etruscan cultural influence remained strong, the Latin cities were politically independent.

The victory at Aricia did not mark an end to Rome's troubles, since the new

constitution was not flawless and there remained powerful external enemies. Internally, one serious threat was the internecine feuding of the leading families, many of whom commanded the support of large numbers of clients and used them on occasion to subvert the power of the state. Another was the struggle between the leading families (the patricians) as a whole and the rest of the population, especially the underprivileged groups (the plebeians). After some years of conflict the plebeians forced the senate to pass a written series of laws (the Twelve Tables) which recognized certain rights and gave the plebeians their own representatives, the tribunes. It was only later, in the 4th century, that plebeians were given the right to stand for the consulship and other major offices of state.

Expansion in Italy

By the 5th century BC, Rome was an important city, but by no means a major regional power. The transition came about only through piecemeal expansion in a series of minor wars. Their earliest enemies were their immediate neighbours to east and south: the Aequi and Volsci. By the end of the 5th century these peoples had been defeated, and the Romans pushed forward their own frontiers, establishing colonies (settlements of Roman citizens) in strategic places. This practice, extensively followed in later years, enabled Rome to hold on to conquered territories and rewarded its citizens with fertile new farmland.

Above: the heart of Republican Rome, seen from the River Tiber. Opening into the river is the mouth of the Cloaca Maxima, the great sewer which drained the valleys between the hills of Rome, making possible the laying out of the Forum. Originally built by the Etruscans, it was substantially repaired during the reign of Augustus (27 BC–AD 14). Above it is the round temple of Hercules Victor, built in the late 2nd century BC.

The first resounding Roman military success was to the north of the city, where in 396 BC after a ten-year siege they captured Veii. This was the southernmost of the Etruscan cities and a major metropolis, in every sense Rome's equal. Any feelings of elation must have been short-lived, however, since six years later Rome itself was sacked by a new and more distant enemy: the Celts (or Gauls). Celtic peoples from Central Europe had been establishing themselves in northern Italy during the course of the 6th and 5th centuries, and in 391 BC a Celtic war-band launched a raid deep into Etruria. They returned the next year in even greater strength, defeated the Romans at the River Allia, and captured the city. The citadel on the Capitoline Hill held out for a few months but eventually capitulated. The Celts withdrew with their booty back to northern Italy, leaving the Romans to pick up the pieces, rebuild the city and restore their damaged prestige. One of their first acts was to provide Rome itself with better defences: the so-called Servian Wall, 6 miles (10 km) long, which was the only city wall that Rome possessed until the Emperor Aurelian built a new one over 500 years later. But it was some years before the Romans were able to return to the offensive.

Whether the Romans entertained any long-term imperialist objectives or merely conquered in self-defence is open to question, but the results were impressive in either case. In 343 they came into conflict with the Samnites, a powerful tribal confederation who controlled the central backbone of southern Italy. This First Samnite War (343–41) was brief and inconclusive, but was followed by more significant Roman gains in the Second and Third Wars (327–304; 298–90 BC). During the same period Rome strengthened its hold over Latium and renewed operations against the Etruscans.

Victory in the Third Samnite War extended Roman territory across the Apennines to the Adriatic Sea. This made Rome a major regional power and attracted hostile attention from the Greek cities around the coast of southern Italy. They called in the help of Pyrrhus, king of Epirus, an ambitious adventurer who arrived at Tarentum in 280 BC with a well-trained army which included war elephants, the first the Romans had encountered. Pyrrhus won battles at Heraclea and Ausculum, but with such heavy loss that they gave him little real advantage. He was eventually defeated in 275, and Tarentum fell to the Romans in 272.

Rome and the Mediterranean

Rome now controlled the whole of the Italian peninsula, either through alliance or direct conquest. The next wars were fought against a much more redoubtable opponent—the Carthaginians—and the prize this time was not merely Italy but the whole of the West and Central Mediterranean.

Rome's principal advantage lay in the enormous reserves of Italian manpower on which it could call. Carthage, on the other hand, was a maritime power with a redoubtable fleet.

Right: *this portrait bust of a Roman aristocrat is believed to represent Lucius Junius Brutus, the founder of the Republic. It dates from the late 4th century* BC.

Right: *the Forum Romanum, first laid out as a public square around 600 BC, was the centre of civic life. Through the middle runs the Sacra Via, Rome's oldest road. In the foreground is Temple of Castor and Pollux, first dedicated in in 484 BC and rebuilt by the future Emperor Tiberius between 7 BC and AD 6. Beyond it is the small round Temple of Vesta. In the background rises the Palatine Hill, on which the emperors later constructed their palace.*

Below: *this statue of a patrician with busts of his ancestors dates from either the 1st century BC or the 1st AD. The patricians were the aristocracy of Rome, and during the later Republic they came increasingly into conflict with senators and generals who took the part of the plebeians. In the late 2nd century BC the brothers Gracchus tried to allocate state lands to poorer citizens, but these reforms gave rise to such hostility that both were murdered.*

The First Punic War (264–41 BC) was fought for control of Sicily. The Carthaginians had long held the western end of the island and had sought from time to time to conquer the Greek cities of eastern Sicily, such as Catana and Syracuse. The cause of the First Punic War, as of many great conflicts, was trivial in origin but revived old rivalries and alerted the Carthaginians to the growing threat from Rome. Despite their seafaring skill, the Carthaginians were defeated by the Romans in a number of naval engagements and by the end of war Sicily was reduced to the status of a Roman province, becoming indeed Rome's first overseas possession.

The Carthaginians were slow to accept their reverse, and in 218 struck back in the Second Punic War, with an invasion of Italy itself, led by Hannibal. This time it was the Romans who were worsted in their chosen element, the land battle, but despite crushing victories at Cannae and Lake Trasimene Hannibal could not shake Rome's hold on the Italian peninsula, and was unable to attack the city itself. In the end the Romans turned the tables by invading Carthaginian territory. Hannibal crossed back to Africa to defend his homeland but was defeated in the final battle of the war, at Zama, by the Roman general Scipio "Africanus" in 202 BC.

The victory over Hannibal removed Carthage as a military threat, but did not bring the Romans any great measure of peace. Instead, they found themselves embroiled in new wars which took them further and further afield. In the west, they became involved in a whole succession of wars in Spain, seeking to protect and expand the territory in the south of the country which they had taken from the Carthaginians. In Italy, close to home, they renewed the conquest of the Celtic lands in the north, which became the province of Gallia Cisalpina (Gaul-this-side-of-the-Alps). But the greatest wars of the 2nd century BC were fought in the Balkans and the East Mediterranean. As the century began, the Romans declared war on Philip, king of Macedonia, and in 196 defeated the Macedonian army at Cynoscephalae. The Romans did not initially seek a lasting foothold in the Balkans, but merely wished to neutralize a military threat. A quarter of a century later they were back fighting a new Macedonian king, Perseus, and by 146 BC had come to realize they had no alternative to direct rule. Greece and Macedonia together became the Roman province of Achaea. In the same year the Romans at last destroyed Carthage, their old enemy, in the Third Punic War; its territory became another new province, Africa. Shortly afterwards, in 133 BC, they gained yet another overseas territory when the last king of Pergamum left his kingdom to the Romans in his will.

Thus, almost by accident, Rome became the ruler of a great Mediterranean empire. The provinces brought wealth to Italy, and fortunes were made through the granting of valuable mineral concessions and enormous slave-run estates. Italian traders and craftsmen flourished on the proceeds of the new prosperity. Slaves were imported to Italy, too, however, and wealthy landowners soon began to buy up and displace the original peasant farmers. By the late 2nd century this process had led to renewed conflict between rich and poor and demands from the latter for reform of the Roman constitution. The background of social unease and the inability of the traditional republican constitution to adapt to the needs of a powerful empire together led to the rise of a series of over-mighty generals, championing the cause of either aristocrats or the poor, in the last century BC.

Below: the Pons Aemilius, the first stone bridge across the Tiber, was built in 142 BC. All that survives today is this one arch, known as the Ponte Rotto.

The Fall of the Republic

The beginning of the end of the Republic came when the brothers Gracchus challenged the traditional constitutional order in the 130s and 120s BC. Though members of the aristocracy themselves, they sought to par-

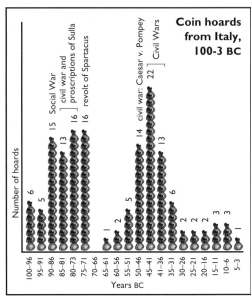

Coin hoards from Italy, 100-3 BC

Number of hoards

Years BC

Above: Republican silver coins—mostly denarii—*of the 2nd and 1st centuries BC. The responsiblility for issuing coins lay with moneyers appointed by the Republic. They put their names on the coins, and often chose designs which reflected their family history. The head of Roma and the four-horsed chariot which appeared on many coins, however, celebrated the city itself.*

Above right: the political conflicts and civil wars of the 1st century BC are reflected in the number of coin hoards buried throughout Italy, Sicily, Corsica and Sardinia, and not recovered by their owners.

cel out public land to the dispossessed Italian peasant farmers. Other measures followed, but many senators came to view the Gracchi as public enemies, and both the brothers met violent deaths.

The next champion of the people was Gaius Marius, a brilliant military commander who reformed the Roman army and saved Italy from the invading Cimbri and Teutones in 102 and 101 BC. He departed from established practice by recruiting his soldiers not only from the landed citizens but from landless citizens, including the growing urban proletariat. These were people who, once the wars were over, looked to their commander for a more permanent reward in the shape of land of their own. Thus the situation developed where commanders and their armies banded together in pursuit of political objectives, the commanders seeking power and the soldiers rewards.

The temporary ascendancy achieved by Marius was eclipsed by that of Sulla in the 80s BC. Sulla made his name in two crucial wars: the first in Italy itself, the so-called Social War of 91–89 BC, where the Italian allies, though they lost the war, largely won their demand for full Roman citizenship; and the second the defeat of Mithridates, king of Pontus, who chose this moment of Roman weakness to overrun Asia Minor and Greece. Sulla was a staunch proponent of aristocratic privilege, and his short-lived monarchy saw the repeal of pro-popular legislation and the condemnation, usually without trial, of thousands of his enemies.

After Sulla's death the pendulum swung back somewhat in favour of the people under a successful new commander, Pompey the Great. He became immensely popular for clearing the seas of pirates and went on to impose a new political settlement on the warring kingdoms of the East Mediterranean, notably making Syria a Roman province. When he returned to Rome in 62 BC he found himself faced by two astute political opponents: the immensely wealthy Marcus Licinius Crassus, and the young but promising Gaius Julius Caesar.

Rather than coming to blows, the three men reached a political accommodation now known as the First Triumvirate. Under the terms of this arrangement Caesar became consul in 59 BC and was then made governor of the two Gallic provinces, one—Cisalpina—south of the Alps, the other—Transalpina—covering the southern part of modern France. He embarked on a campaign of conquest, the Gallic War, which resulted in a huge accession of new territory, and then used his battle-hardened army to overthrow Pompey and take supreme power for himself. Caesar's career was cut short by his assassination at Rome in 44 BC, but rule by one man was becoming an increasingly inevitable prospect. It was a prospect brought to fruition by Octavian, Caesar's adoptive son. He and Mark Antony, Caesar's friend and lieutenant, defeated Caesar's assassins at the Battle of Philippi in 42 BC. They then established the Second Triumvirate, joining forces with Marcus Aemilius Lepidus to divide power between them. The arrangement did not last, however, and eventually resolved itself into direct military conflict between Octavian and Mark Antony. Octavian's victory at the battle of Actium left him sole ruler, and in 27 BC the Senate granted him the title Augustus, making him the first official emperor of Rome.

Below: Greece became a Roman province in the middle of the 2nd century BC. The Roman market at Athens (seen here) was built in the time of Julius Caesar and Augustus. The octagonal Tower of the Winds beyond it was also built during the period of Roman domination, in the mid-1st century BC. Decorated with reliefs of the eight winds, it was originally topped by a weather vane. Inside was a water clock, or horologium.

The Origins of Rome

The early centuries saw Rome grow from a cluster of hilltop farms into a walled city with temples and a paved forum.

"How, then, could Romulus have acted with a wisdom more divine, both availing himself of all the advantages of the sea and avoiding its disadvantages, than by placing his city on the bank of a never-failing river whose broad stream flows with unvarying current into the sea?"

Cicero,
Republic

Tradition held that Rome was founded in 754 BC by twin boys, Romulus and Remus, who were abandoned by their parents but suckled by a she-wolf. Archaeology has revealed that the city actually began life in the 9th or 8th century BC as a series of small farmsteads on a group of hills overlooking the River Tiber. Between the hills were marshy valleys where the local people buried their dead in cemeteries of cremations or inhumations. Early houses, such as the so-called "Hut of Romulus", preserved as a pattern of postholes on the Palatine, would probably have had walls of wattle and daub, and thatched roofs. This early settlement may well have flourished, situated as it was overlooking a convenient crossing point on the Tiber and astride the important salt route running inland from the river mouth.

The crucial development came in the later 7th century BC, when an Etruscan dynasty, the Tarquins, took control of Rome and began its transformation from village into city. The Forum valley was drained by the canalization of the Cloaca Maxima, and was converted into a public square with a gravel paved surface. A wooden bridge, the Pons Sublicius, was thrown across the Tiber, and an Etruscan-style temple to Jupiter Capitolinus built on the Capitol. There may also have been an *agger*, or city wall, with a defensive ditch beyond it, though the oldest defence which survives today (the so-called Servian Wall) dates only from the 4th century BC.

Roman historians maintained that the Romans evicted their last Etruscan king, Tarquin the Proud, in 510 BC, and became a republic governed by a pair of annually elected magistrates, the consuls. It was a momentous step, the first in a sequence which was to take Rome in less than five centuries from small Italian town to mistress of the Mediterranean.

Right: *the she-wolf which suckled Romulus and Remus became the symbol of Rome, appearing in statuary, relief carving and on coins from Republican times on. This bronze figure is believed to be the one set up in the Capitol by the aedile Ogulnius in 296 BC, although its Etruscan workmanship suggests that it was made several centuries earlier.*

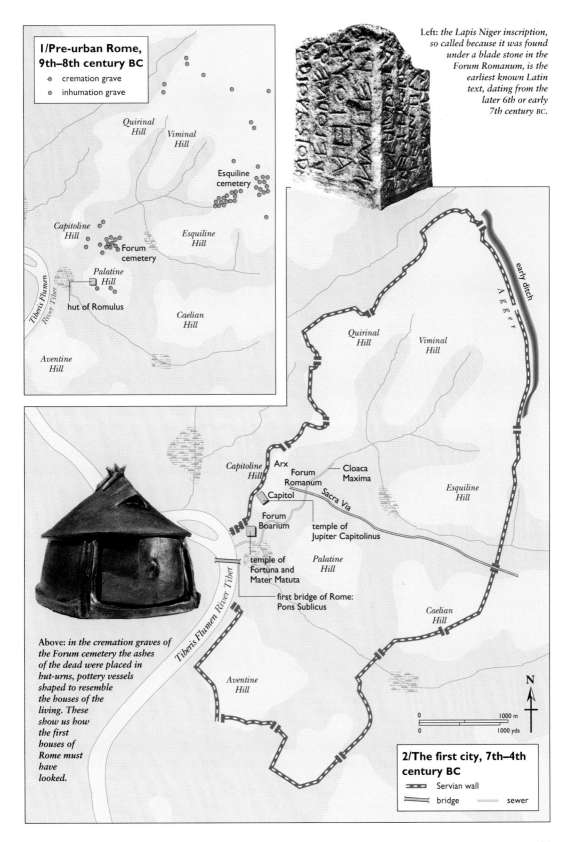

1/Pre-urban Rome, 9th–8th century BC

- cremation grave
- inhumation grave

Quirinal
Hill

Viminal
Hill

Esquiline
cemetery

Capitoline
Hill

Esquiline
Hill

Forum
cemetery

Palatine
Hill

Tiberis Flumen
River Tiber

hut of Romulus

Caelian
Hill

Aventine
Hill

Left: *the Lapis Niger inscription,*
so called because it was found
under a blade stone in the
Forum Romanum, is the
earliest known Latin
text, dating from the
later 6th or early
7th century BC.

early ditch

A g g e r

Quirinal
Hill

Viminal
Hill

Esquiline
Hill

Capitoline
Hill

Arx

Forum
Romanum

Cloaca
Maxima

Capitol

Sacra Via

Forum
Boarium

temple of
Jupiter Capitolinus

temple of
Fortuna and
Mater Matuta

Palatine
Hill

first bridge of Rome:
Pons Sublicus

Caelian
Hill

Tiberis Flumen River Tiber

Aventine
Hill

Above: *in the cremation graves of*
the Forum cemetery the ashes
of the dead were placed in
hut-urns, pottery vessels
shaped to resemble
the houses of the
living. These
show us how
the first
houses of
Rome must
have
looked.

N

| 0 | | | 1000 m |
| 0 | | | 1000 yds |

2/The first city, 7th–4th century BC

- Servian wall
- bridge
- sewer

The Unification of Italy

The Roman conquest of Italy was slow and hard-fought, but by the middle of the 3rd century BC, they were masters of the peninsula.

Right: *this 3rd-century BC pottery dish from Campania shows an Indian elephant equipped for war—probably one of the 20 brought to Italy by Pyrrhus, which would have been the first the Romans had seen.*

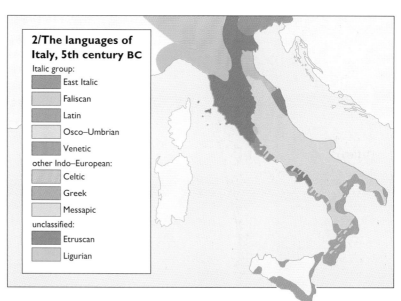

Below: *this ivory plaque, one of a pair from Palestrina in Italy, gives a good impression of the armour and equipment used by Roman soldiers in the 3rd century BC.*

From the early days of the Republic, Rome behaved as an expansionist power, fighting frequent wars to gain new territory and safeguard its security. The first major gain was the capture of Veii, the southernmost of the Etruscan cities, in 396 BC. Any elation was shortlived, however, as six years later a Celtic raiding party descended from northern Italy, defeated the Romans at the River Allia and captured and sacked Rome itself. This proved merely a temporary setback, and during the rest of the 4th century BC the Romans steadily expanded their political and military influence through central Italy. They did this by an astute mixture of warfare and diplomacy, fighting only where necessary. They also adopted a policy of founding Roman colonies at strategic placcs to consolidate their hold on newly conquered territory.

The Romans gained mastery of Latium in the Latin war of 340–38 BC, and then defeated their erstwhile allies the Samnites in the Second and Third Samnite Wars of 327–304 and 298–90 BC. This extended their power east to the Adriatic and southwards to the Bay of Naples. Their next major war was against a foreign invader, Pyrrhus, King of Epirus in northwest Greece. In 280 he landed in southern Italy with an army of 25,000 men and 20 elephants, the first the Romans had encountered. Despite several victories, Pyrrhus was unable to make significant headway and withdrew back to Epirus five years later. This left the Romans free to consolidate their hold on southern Italy, and cast their eyes across the straits to Sicily where, in 264, they came into direct conflict with the Carthaginians (▶ *pages 24–25*).

2/The languages of Italy, 5th century BC

Italic group:

- East Italic
- Faliscan
- Latin
- Osco–Umbrian
- Venetic

other Indo–European:

- Celtic
- Greek
- Messapic

unclassified:

- Etruscan
- Ligurian

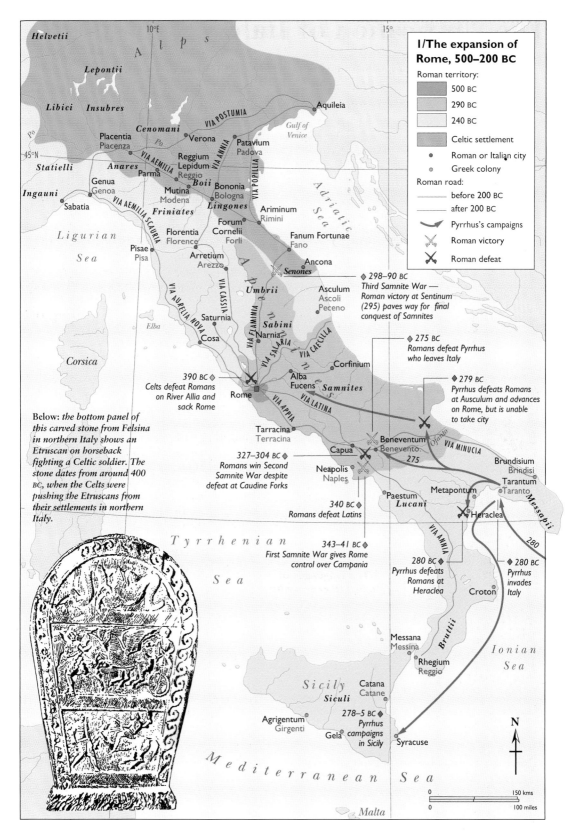

I/The expansion of Rome, 500–200 BC

Roman territory:
- 500 BC
- 290 BC
- 240 BC
- Celtic settlement

● Roman or Italian city
● Greek colony

Roman road:
— before 200 BC
— after 200 BC

⌒ Pyrrhus's campaigns
✗ Roman victory
✗ Roman defeat

Helvetii

Lepontii

A l p s

Libici *Insubres*

Cenomani

Placentia
Piacenza

Verona

Patavium
Padova

Gulf of
Venice

Aquileia

VIA POSTUMIA

Po

Statielli

Anares

Reggium
Lepidum
Reggio

Parma

Boii

Mutina
Modena

Bononia
Bologna

Lingones

Ariminum
Rimini

VIA AEMILIA

VIA ANNIA

VIA POPILLIA

Genua
Genoa

Ingauni

Sabatia

Friniates

VIA AEMILIA SCAURIA

Forum
Cornelii
Forli

Fanum Fortunae
Fano

Florentia
Florence

Ancona

L i g u r i a n

S e a

Pisae
Pisa

Arretium
Arezzo

Senones

A d r i a t i c
S e a

◆ 298–90 BC
*Third Samnite War —
Roman victory at Sentinum
(295) paves way for final
conquest of Samnites*

Corsica

VIA AURELIA NOVA

VIA CASSIA

Umbrii

Saturnia

Elba

Cosa

VIA FLAMINIA

Narnia

Sabini

VIA SALARIA

Asculum
Ascoli
Peceno

VIA CAECILIA

Corfinium

◆ 275 BC
*Romans defeat Pyrrhus
who leaves Italy*

✗
390 BC ◆
*Celts defeat Romans
on River Allia and
sack Rome*

Rome

Alba
Fucens

Samnites

VIA APPIA

VIA LATINA

◆ 279 BC
*Pyrrhus defeats Romans
at Ausculum and advances
on Rome, but is unable
to take city*

✗

*Below: the bottom panel of
this carved stone from Felsina
in northern Italy shows an
Etruscan on horseback
fighting a Celtic soldier. The
stone dates from around 400
BC, when the Celts were
pushing the Etruscans from
their settlements in northern
Italy.*

Tarracina
Terracina

Capua

327–304 BC ◆
*Romans win Second
Samnite War despite
defeat at Caudine Forks*

Neapolis
Naples

Beneventum
Benevento

Ofanto

VIA MINUCIA

275

Brundisium
Brindisi

Tarantum
Taranto

Messapii

Metapontum

Paestum
Lucani

VIA ANNIA

Heraclea

280

340 BC ◆
Romans defeat Latins

T y r r h e n i a n

S e a

343–41 BC ◆
*First Samnite War gives Rome
control over Campania*

280 BC ◆
*Pyrrhus defeats
Romans at
Heraclea*

Croton

◆ 280 BC
*Pyrrhus
invades
Italy*

Brutii

I o n i a n

S e a

Messana
Messina

Rhegium
Reggio

S i c i l y

Siculi

Catana
Catane

278–5 BC ◆
*Pyrrhus
campaigns
in Sicily*

Syracuse

N

Agrigentum
Girgenti

Gela

M e d i t e r r a n e a n   S e a

0   150 kms
0   100 miles

Malta

The Wars with Carthage

Rome's expansion into southern Italy brings it into conflict with the other major power in the Central Mediterranean: Carthage.

By the 3rd century BC, Carthage had become the centre of a maritime empire stretching along the coasts of southern Spain and North Africa and including the western part of Sicily. The major enemies of the Carthaginians had for many years been the Greek cities of Sicily and southern Italy, and Sicily had become a frequent battleground between the two sides.

Rome was sucked into the Sicilian quarrel in 264 BC when Italian mercenaries at Messina called for their help against the Carthaginians. To counter the powerful Carthaginian navy, the Romans had to build their own fleet. They were successful against the Carthaginians on land at Agrigentum (262) and at sea off Mylae (260) and Ecnomus (256), but their invasion of Africa was a disaster, and their fleet was destroyed at Drepana in 249. Eight more years of war followed before the Romans won a final victory in a sea battle off the Aegates islands.

Victory in the First Punic War gave the Romans control of Sicily, but did not deter the Carthaginians from launching a second war, directed at Rome itself, in 218. The leader of the Carthaginian forces was Hannibal, who marched his army from southern Spain across the Alps into northern Italy, defeating the Roman armies sent against him. For 16 years he campaigned in central and southern Italy, winning crushing set-piece battles at Lake Trasimene and Cannae. Hannibal could not capture Rome itself, however, and although at the height of his success much of southern Italy defected to him, he was unable to break the Romans' hold on the peninsula. At last, in 203, he was forced to return to Africa to defend Carthage itself against a Roman counter-attack. His defeat by the Roman general Scipio at Zama in 202 brought the Second Punic War to an end and confirmed Rome's standing as the regional superpower.

Above: this portrait bust, found near Naples, is believed to be of Hannibal (247–183 BC), although the workmanship dates from the 2nd century AD. A talented military strategist, Hannibal was the son of Hamilcar Barca, who had conquered Spain for the Carthaginians.

Opposite: Carthage was founded in the 9th century BC by Phoenician traders and grew into the capital of a powerful maritime empire. This street of substantial, well-built houses dates from shortly after the Second Punic War, testimony to its continued prosperity.

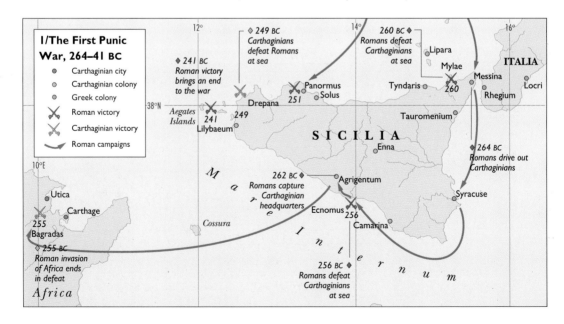

I/The First Punic War, 264–41 BC
- ● Carthaginian city
- ● Carthaginian colony
- ● Greek colony
- ✕ Roman victory
- ✕ Carthaginian victory
- ⟶ Roman campaigns

◆ 249 BC Carthaginians defeat Romans at sea

◆ 241 BC Roman victory brings an end to the war

260 BC ◆ Romans defeat Carthaginians at sea

Lipara

Mylae 260

Messina

ITALIA

Locri

Rhegium

Panormus Solus

Tyndaris

Drepana 251

Aegates Islands 241 249

Lilybaeum

Tauromenium

SICILIA

Enna

◆ 264 BC Romans drive out Carthaginians

262 BC ◆ Romans capture Carthaginian headquarters

Agrigentum

Syracuse

Ecnomus 256

Cossura

Camarina

Utica

Carthage

255 Bagradas

◆ 255 BC Roman invasion of Africa ends in defeat

Africa

256 BC ◆ Romans defeat Carthaginians at sea

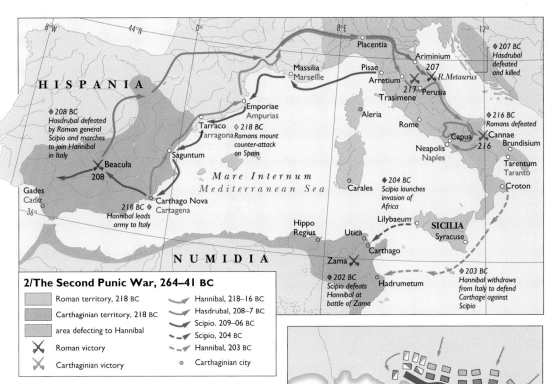

2/The Second Punic War, 264–41 BC

- Roman territory, 218 BC
- Carthaginian territory, 218 BC
- area defecting to Hannibal
- ✗ Roman victory
- ✗ Carthaginian victory
- ➤ Hannibal, 218–16 BC
- ➤ Hasdrubal, 208–7 BC
- ➤ Scipio. 209–06 BC
- ➤ Scipio, 204 BC
- ➤ Hannibal, 203 BC
- ○ Carthaginian city

Map labels:
- 208 BC Hasdrubal defeated by Roman general Scipio and marches to join Hannibal in Italy
- 218 BC Romans mount counter-attack on Spain
- Beacula 208
- 218 BC Hannibal leads army to Italy
- Carthago Nova Cartagena
- Saguntum
- Tarraco Tarragona
- Emporiae Ampurias
- Gades Cadiz
- HISPANIA
- Massilia Marseille
- Placentia
- Ariminium
- 207 BC Hasdrubal defeated and killed
- 207 R.Metaurus
- Pisae
- Arretium
- Perusia
- 217 Trasimene
- Aleria
- Rome
- Capua
- 216 BC Romans defeated
- Cannae 216
- Brundisium
- Neapolis Naples
- Tarentum Taranto
- Croton
- Mare Internum Mediterranean Sea
- Carales
- 204 BC Scipio launches invasion of Africa
- Lilybaeum
- SICILIA Syracuse
- Hippo Regius
- Utica
- Carthago
- NUMIDIA
- Zama
- 202 BC Scipio defeats Hannibal at battle of Zama
- Hadrumetum
- 203 BC Hannibal withdraws from Italy to defend Carthage against Scipio

3/The Battle of Lake Trasimene, 217 BC
- Hannibal's lines
- Roman lines
- Lake Trasimene

4/ The Battle of Cannae, 216 BC
- Hannibal's lines
- Roman lines
- Gauls/Spaniards
- Heavy cavalry
- Africans
- Africans
- Light cavalry
- First Phase
- Second Phase

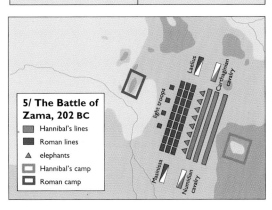

5/ The Battle of Zama, 202 BC
- Hannibal's lines
- Roman lines
- ▲ elephants
- Hannibal's camp
- Roman camp
- Laelius
- Carthaginian cavalry
- light troops
- Masinissa
- Numidian cavalry

Rome's Conquest of the East

In the space of a century, Rome became the dominant political and military power in the eastern Mediterranean.

Above: the ruins of the temple of Apollo at Corinth. The sack of the city by the Roman general Mummius in 146 BC sent shock waves through the Greek world. The historian Pausanias recorded that "the majority... were put to the sword by the Romans, but the women and children Mummius sold into slavery." Mummius became rich on the proceeds, and built a temple to the god Hercules at Rome.

From the end of the 4th century BC, the eastern Mediterranean was dominated by the Hellenistic states which Alexander the Great's generals had carved out of his empire after his death: Macedonia; the Ptolemaic kingdom of Egypt; the Seleucid realm and, in the 3rd century, Pergamum. In theory, the Seleucid kings ruled a vast empire stretching from the Aegean to Afghanistan, but in practice their control was weak and patchy.

Rome entered into eastern politics at the time of the Second Punic War, when King Philip V of Macedon made an alliance with Hannibal. To contain Philip's ambitions on the Dalmatian coast, the Romans went to war in 214 and again in 200, winning a crushing victory at Cynoscephalae in 197. This was their first success over the formidable formation of spearmen known as the Macedonian phalanx. Five years later the Romans became involved in a still more distant war when the king of Pergamum appealed for help against his eastern neighbour, the Seleucid ruler Antiochus III. The Romans crushed Antiochus's land army at Magnesia in 190.

The legions were back in action in Macedonia 20 years later, this time against Philip's son Perseus. At the battle of Pydna in 168 the Romans won a decisive victory and reduced Macedonia to a Roman province. Greece was added in 146, after a war in which the Romans destroyed the leading Greek city, Corinth. Rome acquired its first territory beyond the Aegean in 133, when the last king of Pergamum bequeathed his kingdom to the Roman people; it became the province of Asia. In 101 Romans established a further province of Cilicia in an effort to stamp out piracy. It was not until the wars of the 1st century, however, that Rome cast its imperial noose around the entire region, from the Black Sea to Syria and Egypt.

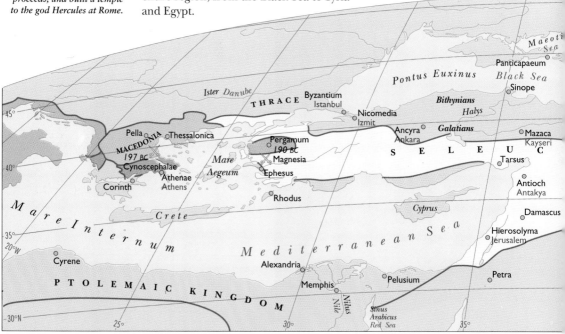

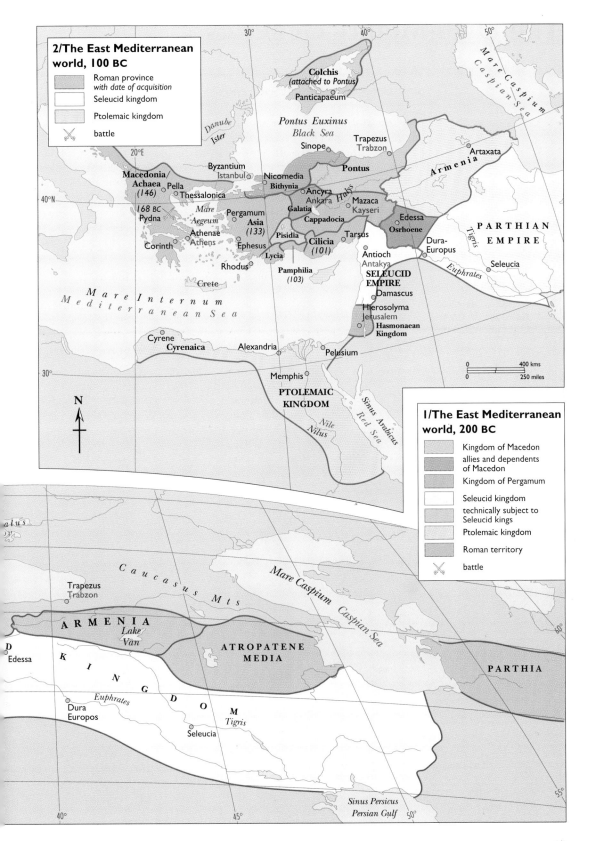

2/The East Mediterranean world, 100 BC

- Roman province *with date of acquisition*
- Seleucid kingdom
- Ptolemaic kingdom
- ⚔ battle

1/The East Mediterranean world, 200 BC

- Kingdom of Macedon
- allies and dependents of Macedon
- Kingdom of Pergamum
- Seleucid kingdom
- technically subject to Seleucid kings
- Ptolemaic kingdom
- Roman territory
- ⚔ battle

The Over-Mighty Generals

In the last century BC a series of generals built up military and political power, pushing the Republic towards dictatorship.

Above: this late republican portrait bust in the Vatican Museum is believed to represent Gaius Marius (c.157–86 BC). After serving with Scipio Aemilianus in Spain, Marius rose through the ranks. He was in his fifties when his victories over the Cimbri and Teutones made him the most powerful man in Rome.

The first of these over-mighty generals was Gaius Marius, who won renown for his victory over King Jugurtha of Numidia and went on to save Rome from the threat of invasion by the Germanic war bands of Cimbri and Teutones. Marius also reformed the Roman army, making it a more disciplined and redoubtable fighting force. His place as leading general was taken by Sulla, who distinguished himself in the Social War of 91–89 BC against Rome's former Italian allies. In 86 BC Sulla moved east to defeat King Mithridates of Pontus, who had taken advantage of the Social War to invade Roman territory in Asia Minor and Greece. When Sulla returned to Rome in 82 BC, he quelled the political opposition and had himself made dictator with absolute power. In 79 BC he abdicated and retired to private life, and died shortly afterwards. This left the field open for younger rivals, including Gnaeus Pompeius Magnus (Pompey the Great). In the 70s BC Pompey campaigned in Spain against the rebel general Sertorius, and in the following decade he reached the peak of his power. In 67 BC he was given an extraordinary command against the pirates who were harrying Mediterranean shipping, and flushed them from their Cilician strongholds. He then went on to inflict a final defeat on Mithridates of Pontus near Nicopolis, and in 64 BC imposed a general settlement on the Near East, making the remains of the Seleucid kingdom the Roman province of Syria, and Judaea a Roman dependency.

OCEANUS
ATLANTIC OCEAN

HISPANIA
77 BC ◆
Pompey sent to Spain to crush rebel general Sertorius; Sertorius murdered by his own officer 72 BC

MAURITANIA

The Roman Empire, 60 BC
Roman territory, 60 BC
✗ Roman victory
✗ Roman defeat
✗ Romans fight Romans
✗ rebellion

Right: this heroic statue of a victorious general was found near Pompey's Theatre in Rome; it may be the one beneath which Julius Caesar was assassinated. Gnaeus Pompeius Magnus (106–48 BC) who built the theatre, was the leading man at Rome until he was challenged by Caesar, pursued to Egypt and killed.

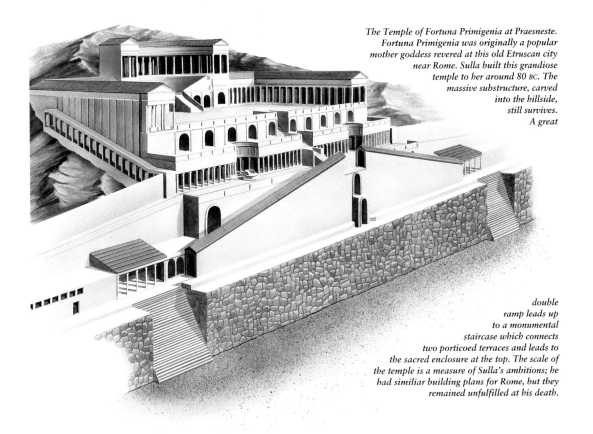

The Temple of Fortuna Primigenia at Praeneste. Fortuna Primigenia was originally a popular mother goddess revered at this old Etruscan city near Rome. Sulla built this grandiose temple to her around 80 BC. The massive substructure, carved into the hillside, still survives. A great double ramp leads up to a monumental staircase which connects two porticoed terraces and leads to the sacred enclosure at the top. The scale of the temple is a measure of Sulla's ambitions; he had similiar building plans for Rome, but they remained unfulfilled at his death.

101 BC ♦
Marius defeats Cimbri

105 BC ♦
d Teutones
man army

Noreia ♦ 113 BC
Germanic war bands of
Cimbri and Teutones defeat
Romans and invade Gaul

Arausio
LLIA Orange   Vercellae
SALPINA ✕Aquae ✕GALLIA
Massilia ✕Sextiae   CISALPINA
Marseilles Aix-en-Provence

♦ 91–89 BC
Social War: Strabo and Sulla
suppress Italian uprising; widespread
grants of Roman citizenship

Ister   Danube

Pontus   Euxinus
Black   Sea

ITALIA   DALMATIA
102 BC ♦   CORSICA   ✕ 73 BC
eats Teutones   Roma   Spartacus launches
Rome   slave rising

ARMENIA
Nicopolis
♦ 66 BC
Pompey defeats Mithridates
of Pontus and receives
submission of Armenians

82 BC ♦   SARDINIA   Capua   ♦ 71 BC
captures Rome   Spartacus killed in battle
omes absolute   in Apulia; survivors crucified
icates in 79 BC   along the Via Appia

MACEDONIA   CAPPADOCIA
ASIA
Mare Pergamum
Aegeum   ♦ 88 BC
Mithridates king of Pontus invades
Roman province of Asia

Halys   Irmak
Tigris

PARTHIAN
EMPIRE

NUMIDIA   Carthage   SICILIA   ACHAEA   Athenae Ephesus
105 BC   Syracusae ♦ 86 BC   Athens
ius Marius defeats   Syracuse   Sulla defeats Mithridates
ng Jugurtha of Numidia   of Pontus at Chaeronea
and Orchomenus

CILICIA   SYRIA   Antioch
♦ 64 BC
Pompey's Eastern Settlement:
Syria becomes a Roman province,
Judaea a Roman dependency

CYPRUS

CRETA
♦ 68–67 BC
Metellus suppresses Cretan
pirates and makes Crete a
Roman province

Mare   Internum
Mediterranean   Sea

JUDAEA   ♦ 67 BC
Pompey suppresses
Mediterranean piracy
and destroys pirate
strongholds in Cilicia

A F R I C A

CYRENAICA   Alexandria
♦ 96 BC   PTOLEMAIC
Cyrenaica bequeathed   KINGDOM OF
to Rome   EGYPT   Nilus Nile

0   450 kms
0   300 miles

N

29

Caesar's Conquest of Gaul

In eight years of dogged fighting, Julius Caesar brought the diverse and independent peoples of Gaul into the Roman Empire.

The conquest of Gaul is one of the best known episodes in Roman history, thanks to the detailed account written by Julius Caesar, commander of the Roman forces. His *Gallic Wars* allows us to follow the progress of the Roman invasion year by year, until eventually the whole of France and Belgium had been transformed into a Roman province.

Julius Caesar was a rising star of the Roman political world when he was appointed governor of northern Italy and southern France in 59 BC. Not content to remain within the boundaries of his province, he quickly embarked on an ambitious campaign of conquest. At first, he posed as an ally of various Gallic peoples, aiding them in their struggles against their neighbours or foreign aggressors. By the second year of his command, however, he had decided to conquer the whole country.

Above: a reconstruction of the fortifications at Alesia, where Vercingetorix made his last stand against the Romans.

Above right: A Gallic coin showing the head of the young warrior Vercingetorix, who led the rebellion against Roman rule in 52 BC. After his defeat he was taken to Rome where he appeared in Caesar's triumph before being strangled.

Despite the popular image, the peoples of Gaul whom Caesar sought to subdue were far from disorganized barbarians. They had coins and kings, towns and trade, and sophisticated craftsmanship in bronze and gold. They put up a fierce struggle, and on more than one occasion came close to inflicting serious defeat on the Roman legions.

Six years of determined compaigning, however, including two celebrated forays to Britain, yielded results. By the winter of 53 BC it seemed as though Gaul was at last conquered. But the greatest test of Roman arms was yet to come, for the following year the Gauls rose up in revolt, led by a young Gallic chieftain, Vercingetorix. The climax came at the siege of Alesia, where Vercingetorix was eventually forced into submission. Gaul was won, and after a further two years' consolidation Caesar was ready to embark on the next stage of his career—the seizure of supreme power in Rome itself.

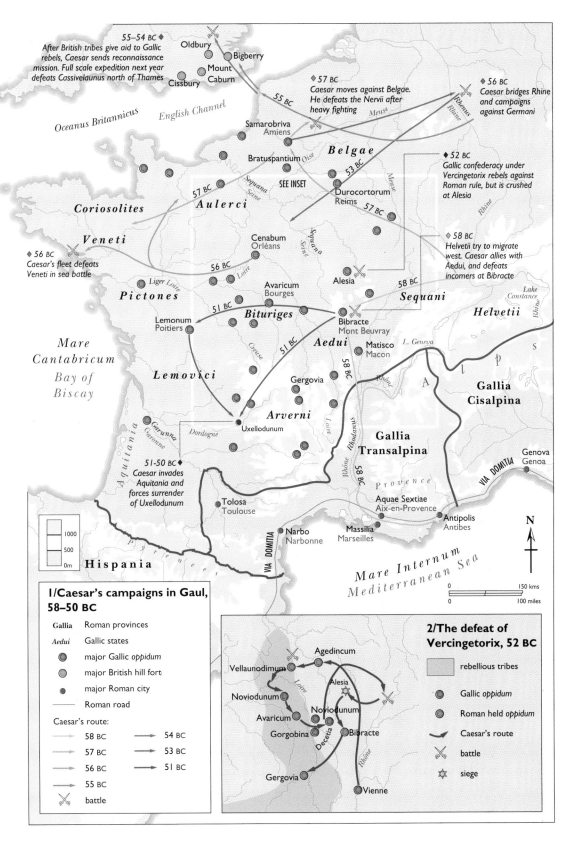

55–54 BC ◆
After British tribes give aid to Gallic rebels, Caesar sends reconnaissance mission. Full scale expedition next year defeats Cassivelaunus north of Thames

57 BC ◆
Caesar moves against Belgae. He defeats the Nervii after heavy fighting

56 BC ◆
Caesar bridges Rhine and campaigns against Germani

52 BC ◆
Gallic confederacy under Vercingetorix rebels against Roman rule, but is crushed at Alesia

58 BC ◆
Helvetii try to migrate west. Caesar allies with Aedui, and defeats incomers at Bibracte

56 BC ◆
Caesar's fleet defeats Veneti in sea battle

51–50 BC ◆
Caesar invades Aquitania and forces surrender of Uxellodunum

Oldbury
Bigberry
Mount Caburn
Cissbury

Oceanus Britannicus
English Channel

Samarobriva
Amiens
Bratuspantium
Oise

Belgae

Durocortorum
Reims

Meuse

Rhenus Rhine

Rhine

Sequana Seine
SEE INSET

Coriosolites
Aulerci

Veneti

Cenabum
Orléans

Sequana Seine

Alesia

Sequani

Lake Constance

Liger Loire
Pictones

Avaricum
Bourges

Bibracte
Mont Beuvray

Bituriges

Lemonum
Poitiers

Aedui

Matisco
Macon

L. Geneva

Helvetii
Rhine
S

Lemovici

Gergovia

Mare Cantabricum
Bay of Biscay

Arverni

Uxellodunum

Dordogne

Garunna Garonne
Aquitania

Loire

Gallia Cisalpina

Gallia Transalpina

Rhodanus Rhine

Rhone

Genova
Genoa

VIA DOMITIA

Tolosa
Toulouse

Provence

Aquae Sextiae
Aix-en-Provence

Antipolis
Antibes

N

Pyrenees

VIA DOMITIA

Narbo
Narbonne

Massilia
Marseilles

Mare Internum
Mediterranean Sea

Hispania

0   150 kms
0   100 miles

1/Caesar's campaigns in Gaul, 58–50 BC

Gallia — Roman provinces
Aedui — Gallic states
● major Gallic *oppidum*
● major British hill fort
● major Roman city
— Roman road

Caesar's route:
→ 58 BC   → 54 BC
→ 57 BC   → 53 BC
→ 56 BC   → 51 BC
→ 55 BC
✕ battle

2/The defeat of Vercingetorix, 52 BC

▨ rebellious tribes

Agedincum
Vellaunodimum
Alesia
Noviodunum
Avaricum
Noviodunum
Gorgobina
Decetia
Bibracte
Loire

Gergovia

Vienne

Rhone

● Gallic *oppidum*
● Roman held *oppidum*
⌒ Caesar's route
✕ battle
✡ siege

Crossing the Rubicon

With a powerful army at his command, Caesar was able to defeat his opponents and make himself the ruler of the Roman world.

"I foresee no peace that can last a year; and the nearer the struggle—and there is bound to be a struggle—approaches, the more clearly do we see the danger of it... Gnaius Pompey is determined not to allow Gaius Caesar to be elected consul unless he has handed over his army and provinces; Caesar on the other hand is convinced that there is no safety for him if he once quits his army..."

Letter from Cicero, Rome 50 BC

The conquest of Gaul saw Julius Caesar at the head of a large and seasoned army, and in 49 BC he led it across the Rubicon into Italy. It was an act of war, since no commander was allowed to take his soldiers outside his province without express senatorial permission, and the River Rubicon was the boundary of Cisalpine Gaul. Caesar marched south to occupy Rome, while the senatorial party opposed to him fled across the Adriatic to Dyrrhachium. There they assembled their own army under the command of Pompey, who was now Caesar's arch-rival. Caesar followed, and laid siege to Dyrrhachium. Pompey broke through his encirclement and withdrew across the Balkans. The two armies eventually met at Pharsalus in Thrace, where on 6 June 48 BC, Caesar won an overwhelming victory.

Pompey fled to Egypt, where he was treacherously murdered, but this did not mark the end of resistance to Caesar. Late in 48 Caesar sailed for

Gallia Transalpina

Galli Cisalpi

Rhenus Rhine

Provincia Romana

Massilia
Marseilles

H i s p a n i a

Corsic

Tarraco
Tarragona

Sardini

Carthago Nova
Cartagena

45 BC

Gades
Cadiz

Munda

♦ 45 BC
Caesar defeats Pompey's sons

Carthage

45

MAURETANIA

Thapsus

The war between Caesar and Pompey, 49–44 BC

Roman frontier, 44 BC

Caesar's campaigns:

49–48 BC

48–47 BC

46 BC

45 BC

siege

battle

N

| 0 | | | 750 km |
| 0 | | 400 miles | |

Egypt where, in the Alexandrian War, he defeated the ruling monarch and placed Cleopatra in control. Then in 47 he marched his armies back to Italy through the eastern provinces. The survivors of Pharsalus had regrouped in North Africa, and in 46 he won a further victory against them at Thapsus. The last sparks of opposition were stamped out in 45 BC when Caesar defeated the army of Pompey's sons at Munda in Spain.

The victory at Munda removed the last of Caesar's enemies in the provinces. Senatorial opposition to the rule of one man was still deeply entrenched, however, and came to a head in February 44 when Caesar had himself appointed perpetual dictator, making him in effect the monarch of Rome. A month later, on 15 March, he was assassinated by a group of senators on the eve of his departure for a campaign against the Parthians.

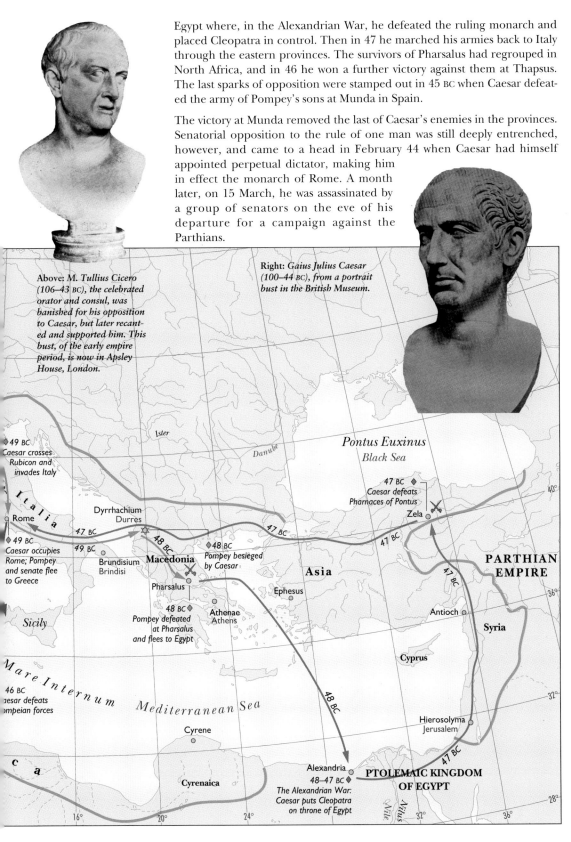

Above: M. Tullius Cicero (106–43 BC), the celebrated orator and consul, was banished for his opposition to Caesar, but later recanted and supported him. This bust, of the early empire period, is now in Apsley House, London.

Right: Gaius Julius Caesar (100–44 BC), from a portrait bust in the British Museum.

49 BC Caesar crosses Rubicon and invades Italy

49 BC Caesar occupies Rome; Pompey and senate flee to Greece

46 BC Caesar defeats Pompeian forces

Ister
Danube
Pontus Euxinus Black Sea

47 BC Caesar defeats Pharnaces of Pontus — Zela

Italia Rome
Dyrrhachium Durres
47 BC
48 BC
Brundisium Brindisi — Macedonia
48 BC Pompey besieged by Caesar
Pharsalus
48 BC Pompey defeated at Pharsalus and flees to Egypt
Athenae Athens
Ephesus
Asia
47 BC
PARTHIAN EMPIRE
Antioch
Syria
Cyprus
Sicily
Mare Internum *Mediterranean Sea*
Cyrene
Cyrenaica
Hierosolyma Jerusalem
Alexandria 48–47 BC The Alexandrian War: Caesar puts Cleopatra on throne of Egypt
PTOLEMAIC KINGDOM OF EGYPT
Nilus

The Civil Wars

The murder of Julius Caesar plunged Rome into a new civil war as his heirs and rivals struggled for supremacy.

Control of the Caesarian party was disputed between Mark Antony and Octavian (Caesar's adopted son). Octavian wanted vengeance for Caesar's death, while Antony favoured reconciliation. Eventually, however, Octavian persuaded Antony to take the field and together they defeated the army of Caesar's assassins Brutus and Cassius at Philippi in 42 BC.

Antony and Octavian agreed to divide effective power between them, Octavian taking the west, and Antony the east, with a smaller third share for their colleague Lepidus. Octavian spent the following years building up his position in the west. In 38 BC he launched a determined effort to capture Sicily from Sextus Pomey, son of Pompey the Great, who had turned the island into a base from which to harrass Rome's grain supplies. It took two years to win and Octavian was then faced with the task of neutralizing Lepidus when the latter attempted to stage a coup against him.

Once Octavian had consolidated his hold on the west he was in a position for a final showdown with Mark Antony. The latter had fallen under

Above: *Marcus Junius Brutus (c.85–42 BC) was a member of the conservative, Republican faction at Rome. He had fought for Pompey against Caesar, and in 44 BC led the conspiracy to assassinate the dictator. After his defeat by Antony and Octavian at Pharsalus in 42 BC, he committed suicide.*

"On this side the commander and soldiers alike were full of ardour; on the other was general dejection; on the one side the rowers were stong and sturdy, on the other weakened by privations ... no one was deserting from Caesar to Antony, while from Antony to Caesar someone or other deserted daily ..."
Vellius Paterculus, *Compendium of Roman History*

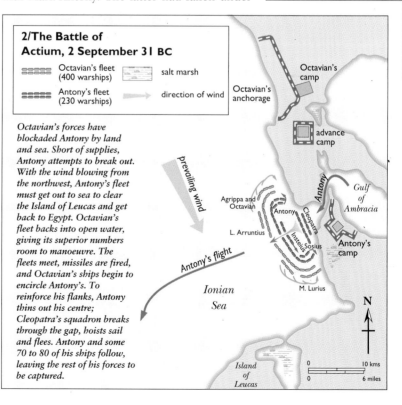

2/The Battle of Actium, 2 September 31 BC

Octavian's fleet (400 warships) — salt marsh
Antony's fleet (230 warships) — direction of wind

Octavian's forces have blockaded Antony by land and sea. Short of supplies, Antony attempts to break out. With the wind blowing from the northwest, Antony's fleet must get out to sea to clear the Island of Leucas and get back to Egypt. Octavian's fleet backs into open water, giving its superior numbers room to manoeuvre. The fleets meet, missiles are fired, and Octavian's ships begin to encircle Antony's. To reinforce his flanks, Antony thins out his centre; Cleopatra's squadron breaks through the gap, hoists sail and flees. Antony and some 70 to 80 of his ships follow, leaving the rest of his forces to be captured.

Octavian's camp
Octavian's anchorage
advance camp
Agrippa and Octavian
Antony
Cleopatra
Insteius Sosius
Antony's camp
L. Arruntius
Gulf of Ambracia
Antony's flight
Ionian Sea
M. Lurius
prevailing wind
N
Island of Leucas
0   10 kms
0   6 miles

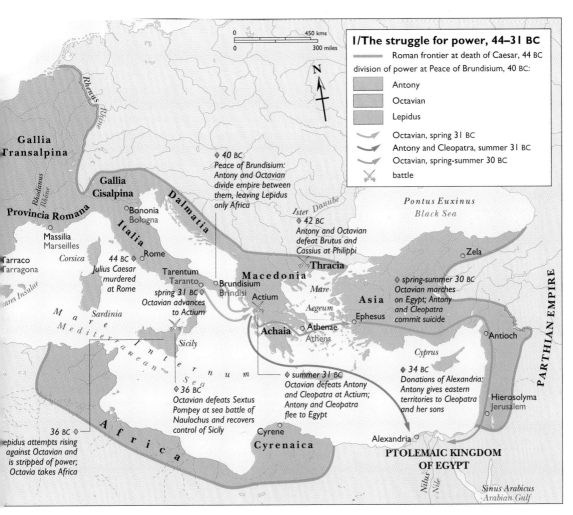

I/The struggle for power, 44–31 BC

Roman frontier at death of Caesar, 44 BC

division of power at Peace of Brundisium, 40 BC:

Antony

Octavian

Lepidus

Octavian, spring 31 BC

Antony and Cleopatra, summer 31 BC

Octavian, spring-summer 30 BC

battle

Rhenus Rhine

Gallia Transalpina

Gallia Cisalpina

Rhodanus Rhône

Provincia Romana

Bononia Bologna

Massilia Marseilles

Tarraco Tarragona

Corsica

Baleares Insulae

Italia

44 BC ◇
Julius Caesar murdered at Rome

Rome

Tarentum Taranto

spring 31 BC ◇ *Octavian advances to Actium*

Dalmatia

◇ 40 BC
Peace of Brundisium: Antony and Octavian divide empire between them, leaving Lepidus only Africa

Ister Danube

◇ 42 BC
Antony and Octavian defeat Brutus and Cassius at Philippi

Thracia

Macedonia

Brundisium Brindisi

Actium

Mare Aegeum

Achaia

Athenae Athens

Pontus Euxinus Black Sea

Zela

Asia

Ephesus

◇ spring-summer 30 BC
Octavian marches on Egypt; Antony and Cleopatra commit suicide

PARTHIAN EMPIRE

Mare Mediterraneum Internum Sea

Sardinia

Sicily

◇ 36 BC
Octavian defeats Sextus Pompey at sea battle of Naulochus and recovers control of Sicily

◇ summer 31 BC
Octavian defeats Antony and Cleopatra at Actium; Antony and Cleopatra flee to Egypt

Cyprus

◇ 34 BC
Donations of Alexandria: Antony gives eastern territories to Cleopatra and her sons

Antioch

Hierosolyma Jerusalem

36 BC ◇
Lepidus attempts rising against Octavian and is stripped of power; Octavia takes Africa

Africa

Cyrene

Cyrenaica

Alexandria

PTOLEMAIC KINGDOM OF EGYPT

Nilus Nile

Sinus Arabicus Arabian Gulf

Right: Mark Antony (Marcus Antonius, 83–30 BC), had served under Caesar in Gaul. After Casesar's death, he took the lead in the Caesarian party, arousing the hostility of Caesar's heir Octavian. The two men were reconciled and formed the Second Triumvirate, an alliance cemented by Antony's marriage to Octavian's sister Octavia. But Antony's relationship with Cleopatra reopened the conflict, leading to his defeat at Actium in 31 BC.

the influence of Cleopatra, Queen of Egypt, who was mistrusted by conservative Roman opinion. The breach came in 32 BC, when Octavian drove Antony's supporters from Rome and declared war on Cleopatra. Antony advanced to Actium on the east side of the Adriatic, where the final sea battle was fought on 2 September 31 BC. After a brief struggle, Antony and Cleopatra fled the scene, yielding outright victory to Octavian. The civil wars ended with their suicide in Egypt the following year. Octavian was now the sole ruler of the Roman world; four years later, in 27 BC, he was granted the title of Augustus, becoming the first Roman emperor.

Shades of the Departed

The funeral monuments of the Romans reflected their belief in an afterlife and indicated the social status of the deceased.

To the Romans the spirits of the dead were known as Manes. There was a common understanding that they remembered with affection their ties with living relatives, and needed to be nourished with offerings of food and drink, and even blood. Some graves had special tubes or openings leading down to the burial for this purpose. Quite where the dead lived was open to differing interpretations. Some thought they descended into the depths of the earth, where they were received by a kindly Mother Earth; others that they lingered near the place where they had been buried; while others believed that they ascended into the heavens.

The main source of evidence for Roman burial customs is the burials themselves, and the funerary monuments (together with their inscriptions) which were erected over them. In general, only wealthy people received carved funeral memorials of stone. These frequently carry a portrait of the deceased (often of several individuals buried in the same family grave) and an inscription addressed to the "Dis Manibus", the spirits of the dead. Burial within the city limits was strictly forbidden by law, and the principal cemeteries grew up along the arterial roads leading from the cities, such as the Via Appia south of Rome. Here, as around other cities, there are a wide variety of tombs from major monuments to simple graves. Special mention must also be made of the catacombs, undergound complexes of rock-cut graves associated with religious communities of Jews and early Christians and found not only at Rome but also at Naples and Syracuse.

Above: a military tombstone from the legionary fort of Virconium (Wroxeter) in Britain. The inscription reads "Marcus Petronius, son of Lucius, of the Menenian tribe, from Vicetia, aged 38, soldier of the 14th legion Gemina, served 18 years, was a standard bearer and is buried here."

The traditional Roman burial rite was divided into several stages. The body was first washed, then anointed and laid out for burial, with a coin placed in the mouth of the corpse to pay Charon the ferryman who would convey the deceased over the river of Styx. On the day of the burial, the corpse would be laid on a funeral couch (for the rich) or a simple bier (in the case of the poor) and carried in procession outside the city or settlement to the place of disposal. Burial itself could take the form of either cremation or inhumation. In Republican times, cremation was the dominant rite at Rome and throughout most of the European provinces, but under the early empire it was steadily replaced by the eastern practice of inhumation until, by the end of the 2nd century AD, even Roman emperors were generally inhumed.

Right: as inhumation took over from cremation as the main method of burial, stone sarcophagi came into use. Only the wealthiest sections of Roman society could afford such beautifully carved sarcophagi as this one, from Aphrodisias in Asia Minor.

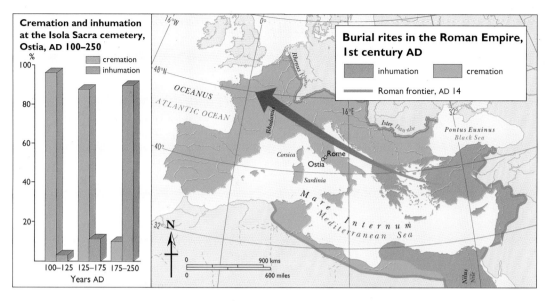

Cremation and inhumation at the Isola Sacra cemetery, Ostia, AD 100–250

- cremation
- inhumation

Burial rites in the Roman Empire, 1st century AD

- inhumation
- cremation
- Roman frontier, AD 14

Some prominent Romans were buried in remarkable grave monuments such as the round tomb of Caecilia Metella beside the Via Appia (right).

Moderately well-off townspeople would have had far simpler memorials; this one (left), from Dyrrhachium (modern Durrës, in Albania), reads "Domitius Sarcinator, from Titia Nicarium the wife of Domitius Sarcinator. Farewell!"

Most people had to be content with a simple pit enclosed by common tiles. Its position would be marked by a pottery vessel (left) into which friends and family could pour offerings of food and drink.

Right: some of the finest examples of Roman sculpture can be found on inhumation sarcophagi of the 2nd and 3rd centuries AD. The exuberant relief carving on this 2nd-century sarcophagus depicts the triumph of Dionysus.

II: The Imperial Regime

The Emperor Augustus gave Rome a stong, centralized government capable of ruling its vast territories, tactfully veiling his power in respect for Republican form. Wealth flooded in to Rome; traders travelled throughout the empire and beyond. Literature flourished and great buildings adorned the cities. Only in moments of crisis, when the succession was unclear, was the underlying power of the military laid bare.

Right: this head of Augustus, from a colossal bronze statue, was found beyond the frontiers of the Roman Empire in Meroe (modern Sudan). It was probably taken from Roman Egypt as booty by raiders from the south.

During the last two centuries BC Rome had become the capital of a great empire, but it was only at the very end of that period that the position of emperor was established. Sulla, champion of the aristocracy, had been absolute ruler of Rome for a few years in the early 1st century BC. Julius Caesar had achieved a similar position in the short period prior to his assassination. Both these had been short-lived experiments, however, and it was only in 27 BC that a constitutional arrangement was reached which gave Augustus supreme power on a regular and agreed basis. And it was only time which showed that this power could be successfully handed on, leading to a long line of Roman emperors from Tiberius, Augustus's immediate successor, to Romulus "Augustulus", the last of the western emperors, almost half a millennium later.

The rise of imperial Rome was not just a question of emperors and armies, however, but was accompanied by an enormous accession of new wealth to Italy. The most populous areas of the Mediterranean world had previously lain in the east, in Egypt, the Levant, and the lands bordering the Aegean (Greece and western Asia Minor). This is not to deny that there had been important Greek colonies and Etruscan cities in Italy and Sicily, nor to ignore the importance of Carthage and its dependancies, but the rise of Rome marks a decisive shift westwards in the economic and political centre of gravity. In one sense, it was a passing phase; by the later Roman period, and throughout the earlier Middle Ages, it was the east once again which was the centre of wealth and power. But during the last centuries BC, and the first two centuries AD, Italy achieved a new level of prosperity which is amply reflected in the remains of cities and villas, and in the production of luxury metalwork and jewellery. Furthermore, Italian merchants and entrepreneurs, stimulated by home demand and sheltered by Roman prestige, travelled far afield in the search for new commercial openings, establishing small colonies as distant as Arikamedu in southern India.

The Augustan settlement

By the 1st century BC it may have become more or less inevitable that Rome should fall under the power of a single ruler. The old Republican institutions were no longer able to cope with the incessant jockeying for power between over-mighty generals, nor could they easily meet the demands of the rapidly growing empire. At the end of the day, however, the position of emperor, and its successful continuation down the centuries which followed, owed much to the wisdom of Augustus. Above all, he succeeded where so great a man as Julius Caesar had failed: in winning acceptance from both the senate and the Roman people at large.

Right: *the* Ara Pacis Augustae *(altar of the Augustan Peace) was set up in the Campus Martius in 13* BC. *The relief depicts the emperor's family; the man with his head covered is probably Augustus's trusted lieutenant Agrippa, the victor of Actium. His young son Gaius clings to his toga. Augustus adopted Gaius and made him one of his heirs, but Gaius predeceased him.*

It was the victory over Antony and Cleopatra at the battle of Actium in 31 BC which gave Augustus supreme power. Learning from Caesar's example, however, he did not seek to enforce his will on the Senate but sought a solution which maintained his position under the cloak of Republican forms. In his personal testament he claimed he had restored the Republic, and in a sense, paradoxically, that was true. Augustus's constitutional arrangement, reached first in January 27 BC and then refined four years later, gave him overall control of the army and most of the important provinces (notably those with military garrisons). It also gave him the power to propose or veto legislation, to overrule any provincial governor, and to sit alongside the elected consuls. For the first nine years, from 31 to 23 BC, he was elected consul as well, but that was not essential to his power base, and later emperors could pick and choose whether they wished to be consul, or allow their supporters that honour instead.

Augustus took particular care to consolidate his position at Rome, and turned the city into a capital worthy of a great empire. He claimed to have found it brick and left it marble, and he and his family beautified it with many new monuments. These included structures of an essentially propagandist or dynastic nature, such as the Ara Pacis Augustae (Altar of the Augustan Peace) or the huge circular mausoleum where he and his close relatives were eventually buried. One notable omission, however, was an imperial palace. Augustus chose to concentrate instead on building public

monuments. Rome by this time had outstripped Alexandria to become the largest city of the western world, with a population of around a million people, and Augustus took particular pains to build new aqueducts and reorganize the regular shipment of grain at state expense on which the urban poor depended.

The imperial succession

Perhaps the greatest of Augustus's legacies were his tactful handling of supreme power and his long life. When he died in AD 14 he had been emperor for over 40 years, and the idea of supreme power in the hands of one man no longer seemed a dangerous innovation. The accession of Tiberius was smoothly handled, and the position of emperor was unchallenged even when he withdrew from Rome to spend much of his last ten years on Capri. Gaius—generally known by his nickname, Caligula—in turn succeeded without serious opposition, but his excesses did raise resentment among the senatorial aristocracy. Both his predecessors had faced conspiracies against their lives—as was only to be expected in an autocratic state—but Caligula was the first to fall prey to such an attempt. Whether he was really madder or badder than other emperors is open to question.

The death of Caligula brought to the fore the power of the praetorians, the emperors' élite corps of bodyguards. However much the senate may have hoped for the return of the Republic, the praetorian guards had a vested interest in the institution of emperor, and appointed the unlikely Claudius, lame and stammering, in Caligula's place. He reigned for 14 years, a period in which the imperial household, and the court officials in particular, became increasingly powerful. That continued under his successor, the notorious Nero. Again, the story of events is strongly coloured by his eventual downfall, but there is no doubt that a reign which began well ran into increasing opposition in later years. His brutal suppression of conspiracy and failure to retain senatorial support undermined his position and led to open rebellion in Gaul and Spain in AD 68. Deserted by his guards and officials, Nero took his own life.

Nero was the last of the Julio-Claudians, the dynasty of emperors who had ruled Rome since Augustus. They were all related to each other, at least by marriage, but it is striking that none was succeeded by his own son. Only Claudius had a son surviving at the time of his death, and he was passed over in favour of Nero. The guiding principal in determining the imperial succession was adoption—Tiberius was adopted by Augustus, and Nero by Claudius.

The death of Nero plunged Rome into a period of crisis, as successive emperors were proclaimed by their supporters, briefly seized power, and then fell before a stronger contender. The year 69 saw no fewer than four of them: Galba, Otho, Vitellius and Vespasian. The major new feature was the role of the frontier armies in promoting their own nominee, and pressing his claims by force where necessary. Thus Vitellius was very much the creation of the Rhine army, and Vespasian came to power through the support of the eastern legions.

The emperors of the later 1st century AD consolidated Roman rule at home and abroad. Vespasian was followed by his sons Titus and Domitian, the only case of direct father-son succession in the whole history of the empire

Above: one of Augustus's acts was to reform the currency, establishing a system which survived until the middle of the 3rd century. The silver denarius (top left) remained the backbone of the coinage, tarrifed at 1/25 of a gold aureus. Its half, the quinarius (next from top) was produced only spasmodically. The large brass sestertius was worth a quarter of a denarius; this one was struck during the reign of Tiberius (AD 14–37). Its half was the brass dupondius, represented here by a coin of Trajan AD 98–117). The radiate crown helped to distinguish it from the similiarly-sized as, which was made of copper and worth half as much; this piece was struck under Gaius— "Caligula" (AD 37–41). The smallest coppers, the semis and quadrans—worth a half and a quarter of an as respectively—succumbed to inflation and were not struck after the early 2nd century.

until the late 2nd century. It was short-lived departure. When Domitian was murdered, the elderly Nerva was chosen by the senate, and he in turn chose Trajan, by adoption, as his son and successor.

The growth of empire

Augustus inherited an empire built up over two and a half centuries of Republican government since the acquisition of Sicily, Rome's first overseas province, during the First Punic War (264–41 BC). There was little planning behind this territorial expansion until the institution of emperor itself created the opportunity for centralized strategic thought. But emperors were expected to be military men, and alongside any grand strategies they recognized the pressure from their subjects to prove themselves successful generals. New conquests also brought slaves and booty, and provided many opportunities for Roman bureaucrats and entrepreneurs to enrich themselves at the expense of the defeated peoples.

Below: this mosaic from the Temple of Fortuna at Palestrina depicts the riches of Egypt that fell into Roman hands after the Battle of Actium in 31 BC. The floodlands of the Nile provided an abundant grain harvest, some of which was shipped to Rome to feed the urban populace. Realizing the political power this gave him, Augustus made Egypt his personal possession; he and his successors ruled it as pharaohs, and no senator was allowed go there without imperial permission.

Augustus himself greatly expanded the empire. His victory at Actium in 31 BC was followed by the invasion of Egypt (whither Antony and Cleopatra had fled for refuge) the following year. Egypt was a large and prosperous country, but under Augustus it became part of the emperor's private domain, a province under his personal supervision. It also provided much of the grain needed to feed the growing population of Rome.

Augustus's major foreign wars were fought with the aim of rationalizing the

Right: *Arabia Petraea was annexed by the Emperor Trajan in* AD *106. Its principal city, Petra, was a major trading centre in the Jordanian desert, famous for its impressive tombs such as the Deir (seen here), which were carved directly from the rock where they stood.*

imperial frontiers. He conquered the northern Balkans, so as to carry the frontier to a suitable natural barrier, the River Danube. Rivers were chosen as boundaries in the east and west as well. In the east, it was the River Euphrates which marked the boundary between the Romans and their eastern neighbours the Parthians. Augustus waged no major wars on this front. It was in the west that the greatest trouble lay. When Caesar conquered Gaul he had made the Rhine the frontier of his new province. That left an awkward salient of unconquered territory in the Alps, between Gaul and Italy. Augustus sought to remove this by conquering the Alpine tribes and carrying the frontier forward here, as in the Balkans, to the Danube. The next step was to move the Rhine frontier forward to the Elbe. That seemed to have been achieved, and the Romans were poised to advance still further into central Europe, when rebellion in the Balkans caused the withdrawal of troops for operations there instead. Three years later, in AD 9, three Roman legions were destroyed by the Germans while crossing the Teutoburg Forest, and the territories beyond the Rhine were abandoned.

Augustus left his successors with the advice not to extend imperial territory, but to consolidate what they already held. There was nonetheless a steady acquisition of new provinces during the 1st and early 2nd centuries AD, driven partly by strategic considerations and partly by the quest for military glory. Sometimes, new provinces were created peacefully by absorbing what had hitherto been client kingdoms. Such was the case with Mauretania in AD 44 and Thrace in AD 46. But other provinces were acquired by direct conquest. The most notable instances are Britain, invaded by Claudius (an emperor desperate for military glory) in AD 43; and Dacia, conquered by Trajan in the two fiercely-fought Dacian wars of 101–2 and 105–6.

The Romans tended to portray their foreign enemies as uncivilized barbarians, but the truth was rather different. The Britain attacked by Claudius was already organized into kingdoms with coinage and towns (though not the kind of market-place coinage in use in the Roman world). Dacia was still more sophisticated, a powerful kingdom with a ruler who had already successfully resisted Roman aggression some 20 years earlier.

The key to Roman military success was of course the army, stationed mainly in camps spread out along the vulnerable frontiers. They had both a defensive and an offensive role, being deployed and redeployed as the needs of individual campaigns or emergencies dictated. One major change from the days of the Republic was the more static conception of the military establishment. It was Augustus who first fixed their pay, and their numbers remained relatively constant, at around 28 legions plus a similar number of auxiliaries, throughout the 1st and 2nd centuries. What did change was the nature of their accommodation, as during the late 1st century the original camps of timber and turf were steadily rebuilt in stone. The frontiers too were strengthened by watchtowers and forts, a first step towards the continuous frontier barriers built by Hadrian.

The rise of the provinces

Within the frontiers, the 1st century was a time of growing prosperity. As the new provinces became better integrated and steadily more Romanized, provincials themselves played an increasingly prominent role in the government of the empire. Roman citizenship was gradually extended to whole towns and cities in the provinces (though always excluding women and slaves), and provincials soon came to form significant minorities in the senate at Rome.

At the same time, the economic balance between Italy and the

Below: the southern parts of Gaul, where Greek colonists had already introduced the trappings of civic life, were quickly integrated into the Roman Empire. The theatre at Arausio (Orange), in Gallia Narbonensis, was built under Augustus; his statue stands in the central niche above the stage.

Right: *Augustus had purchased a villa on the Palatine before he became emperor, and his successors gradually bought up much of the rest of the hill. The surviving ruins are largely the work of the Flavian emperor Domitian (81–96), who built an extensive palace combining state rooms, gardens and private apartments. This transformation of the Palatine Hill into an imperial residence has given rise to the modern word "palace".*

provinces began to change, as the latter began to benefit from the opportunities offered by Roman rule. At one level, the empire was an enormous trading zone where import taxes were held to a minimum. African olive oil and Gaulish Samian ware could now easily be shipped to markets in Italy and beyond, along with the highly prized garum (fish sauce) from Spain. This was a trade in everyday items, not expensive luxuries, and helped to give the whole empire a feeling of community, even though important differences still remained between the east (where Greek was spoken) and the west (where Latin was now the official language).

Trading opportunities were not restricted to the empire itself, however, but extended far beyond. This was especially true in the east, where merchants from the Roman Empire (mostly from Greece or the eastern provinces) sailed the Indian Ocean or travelled the Silk Route to bring eastern luxuries such as Chinese silks or exotic spices and perfumes to the markets of the East Mediterranean. Roman pottery and glassware travelled east in return, but it was gold and silver coins which provided the main means of payment, draining the empire of an estimated 100 million sesterces every year.

The imperial legacy

To the modern observer, the legacy of imperial Rome resides mainly in its literature and monuments. In literary terms, the 1st century AD was part of the golden age of Latin writing which had begun with authors such as Cicero and Catullus in the late Republic. Augustus considered patronage of the arts to be one of the duties of his role as first citizen, and gave support and encouragement to Horace, Virgil and Livy. Other wealthy Romans added their patronage of the poets and historians of the day. The greatest literary work was without doubt Virgil's Aeneid, an epic poem which retold the origins of Rome in the legend of Aeneas fleeing the sack of Troy to make a new beginning in Italy. Other literature took a more practical slant. There were for instance the Natural History, an enormous encyclopaedia by Pliny the elder, who died in the eruption of Vesuvius in AD 79, and the ten books On Architecture by Vitruvius, which exerted such influence on the architects of the Renaissance. There was even a treatise on the Roman water supply. In historical terms, however, our knowledge of the 1st century comes mainly from historians who were writing after its close, above all Tacitus and Suetonius.

In terms of buildings and other monuments, the 1st and early 2nd centuries have left ample remains, including some of the most impressive achievements of Roman architecture. Rome itself saw an upsurge of building under the early emperors. This included a series of adjoining imperial fora (public squares with temples, offices and law courts), supplementing the facilities of the original Forum Romanum at the heart of the city. The last and greatest of these, the Forum of Trajan, is notable today for the striking Trajan's Column, with its spiral relief record of the emperor's Dacian Wars. Mention must also be made of the Colosseum, the largest amphitheatre of the Roman world, which was dedicated in AD 80. The legacy of the early empire extends far beyond Rome itself, however, and includes buildings both public and practical. The great arched aqueducts of Nîmes and Segovia belong to this period, as do the artificial harbours at Ostia and Caesarea. It is these, as much as the monuments of the emperors themselves, which convey the confidence and power of Rome at its apogee.

Below: Trajan's Markets at Rome. In the foreground are the foundations of his forum. The largest of all the Imperial Fora, it contained law courts, offices and, above all, the enormous Basilica Ulpia, now largely buried beneath the Via dei Fori Imperiali. Both Forum and markets were built with the proceeds of Trajan's conquest of Dacia.

The New Order

The Emperor Augustus imposed a new unity on the Roman world, but victory escaped him in Germany.

> *"Augustus kept for himself all the more vigorous provinces —those that could not be safely administered by an annual governor ... He nearly always restored kingdoms he had conquered to their defeated dynasties ... linking together his royal allies by mutual ties of friendship and intermarriage ..."*
>
> Suetonius,
> *Life of Augustus*

In 31 BC Octavian defeated Mark Antony at Actium and became undisputed master of the Roman world. Four years later he reached a constitutional settlement with the Senate at Rome which gave him the title "Augustus" and made him the first Roman emperor. Under this agreement, the provinces were divided into two categories. Those which were considered peaceful were left in the control of senatorial governors; while in frontier and other provinces where military action might still be needed, Augustus chose his own nominees to govern them. He also retained control of Egypt, the wealthy kingdom which he had conquered the year after Actium, and which came to provide most of the grain for Rome's urban populace.

Augustus's foreign wars were undertaken to strengthen the frontiers. Northern Spain was brought under effective Roman rule, while in the Alps and the Balkans the frontier was carried northward to the Danube. The most serious setback was in Germany, where Augustus resolved to create a new frontier on the River Elbe. His stepson Drusus fought a series of successful campaigns between 12 and 9 BC, and by AD 6 the Roman armies (under Drusus's brother Tiberius) were poised to invade the kingdom of the Marcomanni and complete their conquest of central Europe. At the last moment a rebellion in the Balkans forced the plan to be shelved, and three years later in AD 9 the Germans ambushed and slaughtered three Roman legions in the Teutoburg Forest. The Roman frontier was pulled back to the Rhine, where it was to stay until the fall of the western empire four centuries later.

Right: Augustus took the security of the empire very seriously, acting as commander-in-chief of the Roman armies. This 1st-century BC statue from the Prima Porta in Rome shows him in full dress uniform, stressing the importance of his military power base.

OCEANUS
ATLANTIC OCEAN

Lugdunensis
Liger
Loire

Burdigala
Bordeaux

Aquitania

Tolos
Toulc

Salamantica
Salamanca

Caesaraugusta
Saragossa

Lusitania

Toletum
Toledo

Na

Narbo
Narbonne

Emerita Augusta
Merida

Tarraconensis

Tarrac
Tarrag

Hispalis
Seville

Corduba

Baetica
Gades
Cadiz

Balea

Tingi
Tangier

Carthago Nova
Cartagena

Caesarea

MAURETANIA

N

0   400 kms

0   250 miles

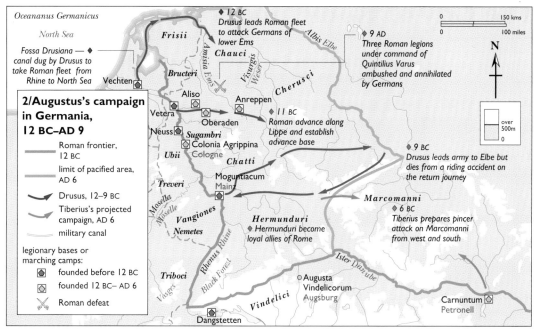

2/Augustus's campaign in Germania, 12 BC–AD 9

Oceananus Germanicus
North Sea

Fossa Drusiana — ◆
canal dug by Drusus to
take Roman fleet from
Rhine to North Sea

◆ 12 BC
Drusus leads Roman fleet
to attack Germans of
lower Ems

◆ 9 AD
Three Roman legions
under command of
Quintilius Varus
ambushed and annihilated
by Germans

◆ 11 BC
Roman advance along
Lippe and establish
advance base

◆ 9 BC
Drusus leads army to Elbe but
dies from a riding accident on
the return journey

◆ 6 BC
Tiberius prepares pincer
attack on Marcomanni
from west and south

Hermunduri ◆
Hermunduri become
loyal allies of Rome

Roman frontier,
12 BC

limit of pacified area,
AD 6

Drusus, 12–9 BC

Tiberius's projected
campaign, AD 6

military canal

legionary bases or
marching camps:

founded before 12 BC

founded 12 BC– AD 6

Roman defeat

Frisii, Chauci, Bructeri, Cherusci, Vechten, Aliso, Anreppen, Vetera, Oberaden, Neuss, Sugambri, Colonia Agrippina, Cologne, Ubii, Chatti, Treveri, Moguntiacum, Mainz, Mosella, Moselle, Vangiones, Nemetes, Marcomanni, Triboci, Vosges, Black Forest, Rhenus Rhine, Augusta Vindelicorum, Augsburg, Vindelici, Ister Danube, Carnuntum, Petronell, Dangstetten, Amisia Ems, Visurgis Weser, Albis Elbe

over 500m

0 150 kms
0 100 miles

N

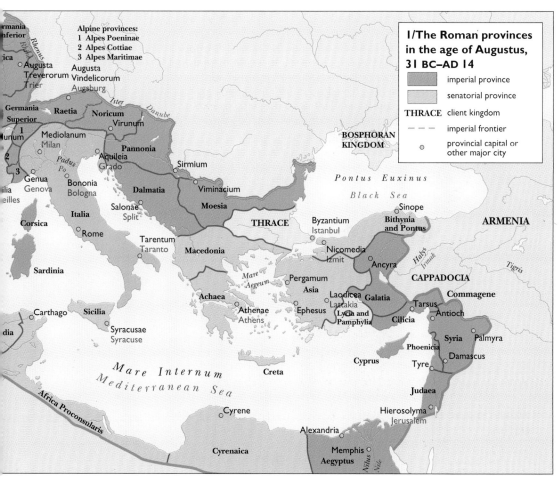

1/The Roman provinces in the age of Augustus, 31 BC–AD 14

imperial province

senatorial province

THRACE client kingdom

imperial frontier

provincial capital or
other major city

Alpine provinces:
1 Alpes Poeninae
2 Alpes Cottiae
3 Alpes Maritimae

Germania Inferior, Germania Superior, Augusta Treverorum Trier, Augusta Vindelicorum Augsburg, Raetia, Noricum, Virunum, Mediolanum Milan, Aquileia Grado, Pannonia, Sirmium, Padus Po, Bononia Bologna, Dalmatia, Viminacium, Salonae Split, Moesia, Italia, Corsica, Rome, Genua Genova, Tarentum Taranto, Macedonia, Sardinia, Carthago, Sicilia, Syracusae Syracuse, Achaea, Athenae Athens, Creta, Africa Proconsularis, Cyrene, Alexandria, Cyrenaica, Memphis, Aegyptus, Nilus Nile, Mare Internum Mediterranean Sea, Mare Aegeum, THRACE, Byzantium Istanbul, Nicomedia Izmit, Pergamum, Asia, Ephesus, Laodicea Lattakia, Lycia and Pamphylia, Cyprus, Tyre, Judaea, Hierosolyma Jerusalem, BOSPHORAN KINGDOM, Pontus Euxinus, Black Sea, Sinope, Bithynia and Pontus, Ancyra, Halys Irmak, Galatia, Cilicia, CAPPADOCIA, Tarsus, Antioch, Commagene, ARMENIA, Tigris, Syria, Palmyra, Phoenicia, Damascus, Rhenus, Ister, Danube

47

The City of Rome under Augustus

Under Augustus, Rome became the greatest city of the western world, graced with impressive new public buildings.

"Since the city was not adorned as the dignity of the empire demanded, and was exposed to flood and fire, he so beautified it that he could justly boast that he had found it built of brick and left it in marble."
Suetonius, *Life of Augustus*

By the end of the 1st century BC, Rome had a population of around a million people, from wealthy senators to craftsmen, shopkeepers and slaves. Realizing that the city's infrastructure had not kept pace with its rapid growth, Augustus divided Rome into 14 administrative regions, each under an appointed magistrate, set up a police force and fire brigade, and built or restored several aqueducts. To prevent flooding he had the River Tiber dredged and widened; according to his biographer Suetonius it had "for some time been filled with rubbish and narrowed by jutting buildings." Crucially, Augustus took personal responsibility for the corn dole, the monthly distribution of free grain to the city's poor.

Augustus also spent enormous sums on the aggrandisement of the city, making it a worthy capital for so great an empire. He boasted that he found Rome brick and left it marble, and the claim was not ill-founded. At the heart of the metropolis, many of the existing buildings of the Forum Romanum were faced in marble for the first time during his reign. Nearby he built his own new Forum to serve as a lawcourt and administrative centre. In his rebuilding of the city, Augustus was assisted by members of his family and by trusted friends and lieutenants such as Statilius Taurus and above all Marcus Agrippa. In the Campus Martius region to the north of the city, Agrippa was responsible for a whole series of new buildings: the original Pantheon, the Baths of Agrippa and the Saepta Julia. North of these Augustus erected an enormous sundial, the Horologium, with an obelisk brought from Egypt as its pointer. Nearby, standing within a park, was the circular Mausoleum, designed to resemble an Etruscan burial mound, where in AD 14 the ashes of Augustus himself were finally laid to rest.

Above: among the many public buildings of Augustan Rome were places of entertainment. The Theatre of Marcellus, completed in 11 BC and named after the emperor's nephew, can be seen here behind the columns of the earlier Temple of Apollo.

Right: the Forum of Augustus was dedicated in 2 BC. Its centrepiece was the temple of Mars Ultor (Mars the Avenger) to commemorate the fact that Augustus had avenged the murder of Julius Caesar. The statues proclaim Augustus's family lineage, going back to the city's legendary founder Aeneas.

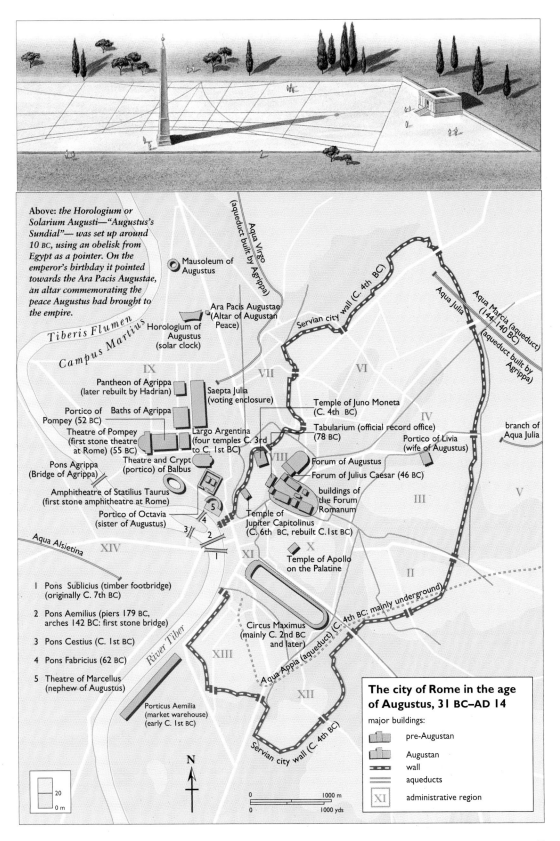

Above: *the Horologium or
Solarium Augusti—"Augustus's
Sundial"— was set up around
10 BC, using an obelisk from
Egypt as a pointer. On the
emperor's birthday it pointed
towards the Ara Pacis Augustae,
an altar commemorating the
peace Augustus had brought to
the empire.*

Aqua Virgo
(aqueduct built by Agrippa)

Aqua Julia

Aqua Marcia (aqueduct)
(144–140 BC)
(aqueduct built by Agrippa)

Servian city wall (C. 4th BC)

Mausoleum of
Augustus

Ara Pacis Augustae
(Altar of Augustan
Peace)

Tiberis Flumen

Horologium of
Augustus
(solar clock)

Campus Martius

IX

VII

VI

IV

branch of
Aqua Julia

Pantheon of Agrippa
(later rebuilt by Hadrian)

Saepta Julia
(voting enclosure)

Temple of Juno Moneta
(C. 4th BC)

Portico of   Baths of Agrippa
Pompey (52 BC)

Tabularium (official record office)
(78 BC)

Portico of Livia
(wife of Augustus)

Theatre of Pompey
(first stone theatre
at Rome) (55 BC)

Largo Argentina
(four temples C. 3rd
to C. 1st BC)

VIII

Forum of Augustus
Forum of Julius Caesar (46 BC)

Pons Agrippa
(Bridge of Agrippa)

Theatre and Crypt
(portico) of Balbus

buildings of
the Forum
Romanum

III

V

Amphitheatre of Statilius Taurus
(first stone amphitheatre at Rome)

5

Portico of Octavia
(sister of Augustus)

4

3

2

Temple of
Jupiter Capitolinus
(C. 6th BC, rebuilt C.1st BC)

X

Aqua Alsietina

XIV

1

XI

Temple of Apollo
on the Palatine

II

1 Pons Sublicius (timber footbridge)
   (originally C. 7th BC)

2 Pons Aemilius (piers 179 BC,
   arches 142 BC: first stone bridge)

Aqua Appia (aqueduct) C. 4th BC: mainly underground)

Circus Maximus
(mainly C. 2nd BC
and later)

3 Pons Cestius (C. 1st BC)

River Tiber

XIII

4 Pons Fabricius (62 BC)

5 Theatre of Marcellus
   (nephew of Augustus)

XII

Porticus Aemilia
(market warehouse)
(early C. 1st BC)

Servian city wall (C. 4th BC)

N

20

0 m

0   1000 m
0   1000 yds

**The city of Rome in the age
of Augustus, 31 BC–AD 14**

major buildings:

pre-Augustan

Augustan

wall

aqueducts

XI   administrative region

49

Claudius and the Conquest of Britain

Above: *this bronze head of the Emperor Claudius (r. AD 41–54) may have come from the temple of Claudius at Colchester. It was found in the River Alde in Suffolk, where it was probably thrown after being torn from a statue taken as booty during Boudicca's revolt.*

"The quarrels of petty chieftains divide them; nor indeed have we any weapon… more effective than this, that they have no common purpose: rarely will two or three states confer to repulse a common danger; accordingly they fight individually and are collectively conquered."
Tacitus, *Agricola*

The Romans invaded Britain in AD 43, and went on to most of the island under direct rule by the end of the 1st century.

Britain was a relatively late addition to the Roman Empire. Julius Caesar had made two expeditions to southern England in 55 and 54 BC, but though he received the nominal submission of several southern leaders there was no follow-up, and Britain lay beyond direct Roman control for another century. It was politics at Rome rather than any military or economic necessity which eventually led the Emperor Claudius to invade the island in 43. Claudius's reign, following the murder of Caligula in January 41, had got off to a shaky start, and he badly needed a military victory to shore up his prestige. The invading force consisted of four legions and was commanded by Aulus Plautius, who became the first governor of Roman Britain. The main army put ashore at Richborough, forced its way across the Medway and the Thames and captured Colchester, capital of the powerful Catuvellaunian kingdom.

During the following years the Romans steadily expanded their control over the rest of southern Britain and into Wales. In 47 they suppressed a rebellion among the Iceni, who had earlier allied themselves with Rome; four years later they defeated and captured the native leader Caratacus. The last serious opposition in southern Britain was the revolt led by Boudicca, queen of the Iceni, in 60–61, which was only suppressed after serious reverses.

At first the Romans attempted to control northern England through their allies, the Brigantes. But in 69 an anti-Roman faction gained control of the tribe, leading to military intervention which brought the area under direct Roman rule. From 79 the famous general Agricola embarked on the conquest of Scotland, and four years later won a great victory over the natives at Mons Graupius. At this point, however, trouble on the Danube frontier forced the emperor Domitian to withdraw troops from Britain and give up the attempt to conquer the whole island. Agricola's conquests were steadily abandoned, and by the end of the century the frontier had been pulled back to the Tyne–Solway isthmus, where Hadrian was to build his wall (▶ *page 86–7*).

Right: *a Roman ballista bolt lodged in the spine of a skeleton buried at Maiden Castle in Dorset. The victim may have been killed during the Roman siege of this hill fort, or in the massacres that followed.*

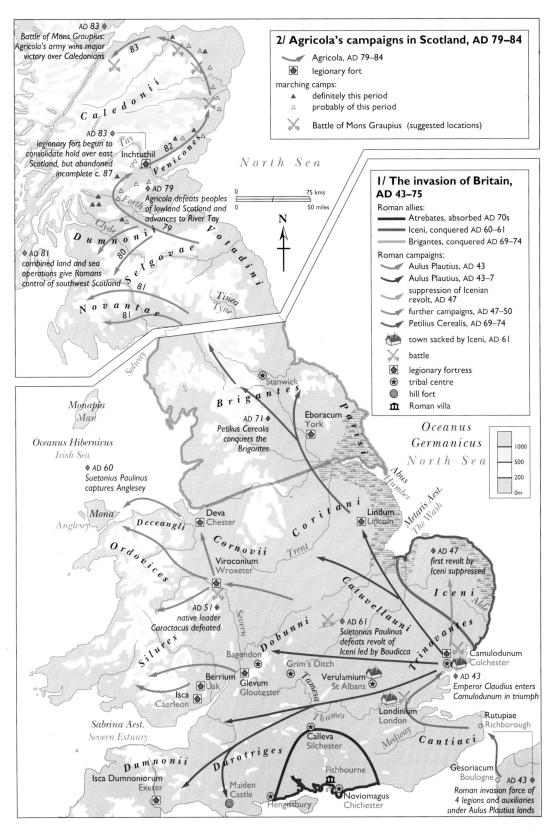

2/ Agricola's campaigns in Scotland, AD 79–84

- Agricola, AD 79–84
- ◈ legionary fort

marching camps:
- ▲ definitely this period
- △ probably of this period

- ✕ Battle of Mons Graupius (suggested locations)

1/ The invasion of Britain, AD 43–75

Roman allies:
- Atrebates, absorbed AD 70s
- Iceni, conquered AD 60–61
- Brigantes, conquered AD 69–74

Roman campaigns:
- Aulus Plautius, AD 43
- Aulus Plautius, AD 43–7
- suppression of Icenian revolt, AD 47
- further campaigns, AD 47–50
- Petilius Cerealis, AD 69–74

- town sacked by Iceni, AD 61
- ✕ battle
- ◈ legionary fortress
- ✷ tribal centre
- ● hill fort
- 🏛 Roman villa

AD 83 ◈
Battle of Mons Graupius: Agricola's army wins major victory over Caledonians

Caledonii

AD 83 ◈
legionary fort begun to consolidate hold over east Scotland, but abandoned incomplete c. 87

Inchtuthil

Tay

Venicones

North Sea

AD 79 ◈
Agricola defeats peoples of lowland Scotland and advances to River Tay

Forth

Votadini

Clyde

Dumnonii

AD 81 ◈
combined land and sea operations give Romans control of southwest Scotland

Selgovae

Tinea Tyne

Novantae

N

0 ____ 75 kms
0 ____ 50 miles

Solway

Monapia Man

Oceanus Hibernicus
Irish Sea

Stanwick ✷

Brigantes

Parisi

Eboracum York ◈

AD 71 ◈
Petilius Cerealis conquers the Brigantes

Oceanus Germanicus
North Sea

1000
500
200
0m

Abus Humber

AD 60 ◈
Suetonius Paulinus captures Anglesey

Mona Anglesey

Deceangli

Deva Chester ◈

Cornovii

Lindum Lincoln ◈

Metaris Aest. The Wash

AD 47 ◈
first revolt by Iceni suppressed

Coritani

Ordovices

Viroconium Wroxeter ◈✕

Trent

Iceni

Alde

AD 51 ◈
native leader Caractacus defeated

Severn

Catuvellauni

Dobunni

AD 61 ◈
Suetonius Paulinus defeats revolt of Iceni led by Boudicca

Trinovantes

Camulodunum Colchester ✷🏛

AD 43 ◈
Emperor Claudius enters Camulodunum in triumph

Silures

Bagendon ✷

Grim's Ditch

Verulamium St Albans ✷🏛

Berrium Usk ◈

Glevum Gloucester ✷

Isca Caerleon ◈

Tamesa

Londinium London 🏛◈

Rutupiae Richborough ○

Sabrina Aest.
Severn Estuary

Thames

Calleva Silchester ✷

Medway

Cantiaci

Dumnonii

Durotriges

Fishbourne 🏛

Gesoriacum Boulogne ○

AD 43 ◈
Roman invasion force of 4 legions and auxiliaries under Aulus Plautius lands

Isca Dumnoniorum Exeter ◈

Maiden Castle ●

Hengistbury ✷

Noviomagus Chichester

Nero and the Year of Four Emperors

Nero's unpopularity brought the rule of Augustus's family to an end, and plunged the empire into civil war.

Nero (r. 54–68) was the last of the Julio-Claudians, the dynasty founded by Augustus. He was only 16 when he succeeded his adoptive father Claudius, but he was guided by able advisers and the first years of the reign were later regarded as a golden age. As time went by, however, there was growing conflict with the senate, and in 65 a wide-ranging conspiracy against Nero was discovered and brutally suppressed. He also became unpopular among the wealthy for confiscating property, and was suspected by many of having intentionally started the Great Fire which destroyed the centre of Rome in 64. The suspicion was untrue, but Nero did not help matters by buying up the land to build his Golden House, a lavish garden villa set in the heart of the capital.

The end came in 68, when first Vindex in Gaul and then Galba in Spain broke out in open rebellion against him. Vindex was quickly defeated, but Nero lost support at Rome and was driven to suicide in June. He was succeeded by the elderly Galba, who arrived in Rome in the autumn of 68 but was murdered in the Forum in January the following year. His murderer Otho seized power at Rome, but the Rhine legions had already declared in favour of their own commander Aulus Vitellius. Otho had relatively few troops at his disposal in Italy and had been defeated by the invading Vitellian forces at the First Battle of Cremona in April. Vitellius now took control of Rome, but by July another rival emperor had been proclaimed in the east: Titus Flavius Vespasianus (Vespasian), commander in the Jewish War. The Danube legions declared for Vespasian and led by Antonius Primus defeated the Vitellians at the Second Battle of Cremona in September 69. In December the Flavian forces fought their way into Rome, dragged Vitellius from his hiding place and killed him, in his turn, in the Forum. Vespasian became undisputed ruler of the Roman world, the fourth and last emperor of the eventful year 69.

Above: the four emperors who followed Nero in rapid succession, as depicted on their silver coins. All were experienced administrators or military men. Galba (top) was the governor of Hispania Tarraconensis and already over 70 when declared emperor. Otho (second from top), a friend and supporter of Nero, had gone over to Galba in the hope of being named as his successor. When Galba appointed someone else, Otho had them both murdered. Soon after, Vitellius (second from bottom) marched on Rome. He seized power, only to be deposed by the supporters of Vespasian (bottom).

Right: a contemporary Roman portrait bust of Nero. Declared a public enemy by the Senate, he fled Rome and committed suicide, aged 31, at the suburban villa of one of his freedmen. According to the biographer Suetonius, his dying words were, "How ugly and vulgar my life has become!" Despite his unpopularity with the Senate and the army, Nero was not without his supporters, who continued to place flowers on his grave for years afterwards.

I/The wars of succession, AD 68–9

- Roman Empire
- provincial capital or major city
- Vindex, Mar–May 68
- Galba, Apr–autumn 68
- Vitellius, Jan–July 69
- Vespasian, July–Dec 69
- battle

Burdigala / Bordeaux
June 68 — Galba learns of Nero's death
Mar 68 — Vindex rebel against Nero and attack
Salamantica / Salamanca
Clunia
Lugdunum
Caesaraugusta / Saragossa
Emerita Augusta / Merida
Toletum / Toledo
Corduba / Cordoba
Hispalis
Gades / Cadiz
Apr 68 — Galba proclaimed emperor
Tingi / Tangier
Carthago No / Cartagena
Caesarea

N

2/Otho v. Vitellius, AD 69
- Otho's forces
- Vitellius's forces
- ✕ battle

3/Vitellius v. Vespasian, AD 69
- Vitellius's forces
- Vespasian's forces
- ✕ battle

Cremona *1,2*
Bedriacum
◆ 12 Apr Otho holds council of war
Placentia Piacenza
Brixellum Brescello
Padus
Bononia Bologna
Mare Adriaticum
Arminium Rimini
late March ◆ Caecina mounts abortive attack on Placentia
◆ 16 Apr Otho commits suicide
◆ Mar–Apr Vitellius's forces invade Italy in two divisions under Valens and Caecina
Fanum Fortunae Fano
Mare Ligusticum
1 ◆ early April Valens joins Caecina
June ◆ Vitellius's forces advance on Rome
2 ◆ 14 Apr Otho's forces defeated
N
0 — 100 kms
0 — 60 miles
17 July ◆ Vitellius enters Rome
Rome
◆ 14 Mar Otho leaves Rome

mid–Aug ◆ Vespasian's supporters entrust Antonius Primus with invasion of Italy
◆ late Aug Antonius occupies Aquileia
Poetovio ○
late Sept ◆ Vespasian's supporters set up camp
◆ 3 Sept Antonius captures Patavium
◆ 17 July Vitellius enters Rome
Aquileia
Cremona *1,2*
Bedriacum
Hostilia
Patavium Padua
◆ Vitellian forces divide: first division to Hostilia, second to Cremona
Verona
Placentia Piacenza
Brixellum Brescello
Padus
Bononia Bologna
Ravenna
Arminium Rimini
◆ 2 Jan 69 Rhine legions declare for Vitellius
Cologna Agrippina Cologne
Rhenus Rhine
◆ 14 Apr 69 first battle of Cremona: Vitellians defeat Otho
◆ 24–25 Oct 69 second battle of Cremona: Vespasian's forces defeat Vitellians
◆ Aug 69 Danube legions declare for Vespasian
Augusta Treverorum Trier
May 68 ◆ Nero's forces defeat Vindex
Vesontio ✕
Lugdunum Lyon
Cremona
Padus Po
Mare Ligusticum
1 ◆ 24–5 Oct Vitellian forces defeated
2 ◆ Vitellians abandon Hostilia and concentrate at Cremona
20 Nov ◆ Vespasian's forces advance to Fanum Fortunae
Fanum Fortunae Fano
Mare Adriaticum
15 Dec ◆ Vitellians attempt to hold Narnia, but surrender Narnia Narni
◆ 17 Sept Caecina leads Vitellian forces from Rome
20 Dec ◆ Vespasian's supporters fight their way into Rome and kill Vitellius
Rome ○
N
0 — 100 kms
0 — 60 miles
Massilia Marseilles
Genua Genova
Bononia Bologna
arbo arbonne
raco ragona
te summer 68 ba sets out Rome
Rome
15 Jan 69 ◆ Otho deposes and kills Galba
20 Dec 69 ◆ Vespasian's forces occupy Rome
Narona
Tarentum Taranto
Byzantium Istanbul
Nicomedia
Ancyra Ankara
Halys Irmak
Mare Aegeum
Pergamum
Laodicea
Tarsus
Antioch
Palmyra
summer 70 ◆ Vespasian travels to Rome to take power
Athenae Athens
Ephesus
Cirta
Carthago Carthage
Syracusae Syracuse
Damascus
Tyre
Caesarea
◆ July 69 Vespasian declared emperor
Mare Internum Mediterranean Sea
Cyrene
winter 69–70 ◆ Vespasian in Alexandria
Alexandria
Memphis
Nilus Nile
Sinus Arabicus
0 — 450 kms
0 — 300 miles

The Western Provinces

Romes's western provinces included a wide range of cultures, from the urban south to the rural Celtic north.

"Today the whole world has its Graeco-Roman culture. Smart Gaulish professors are training the lawyers of Britain…"
Juvenal,
Satire XV

The southwestern provinces of the Roman Empire were the rich Mediterranean regions of Spain (▶ *pages 84–5*), southern France, and Italy itself, where city life had been established long before the spread of Roman rule. Further north, in Gaul, Britain and the Germanies, were the less urbanized lands of the Celts and others. To all these regions Roman rule brought certain benefits—notably peace and wider trading opportunities—and the western provinces steadily took on more and more of the trappings of Roman culture. New cities were founded with grid-plan street layouts, classical temples and municipal baths. Amphitheatres were built in or beside the major towns, supplemented by theatres in the more literate south. Elaborate aqueducts provided fresh drinking water to the cities, while roads and bridges ensured better communications.

The provinces soon became closely incorporated in the imperial system itself; the Emperor Claudius gave leading Gaulish citizens the right to became senators at Rome, and the spread of power from Italy to the provinces continued in the centuries which followed. Britain and the Germanies also took a leading part in the political life of the empire through the size of their military garrisons: three to four legions in Britain and eight (later reduced to four) along the Rhine, supported by substantial auxiliary forces. It was the Rhine legions which backed Vitellius's bid for power in AD 69 (▶ *pages 52–3*), and the army of Britain which supported Clodius Albinus in the 190s (▶ *pages 96–7*). The most telling legacy of Roman rule, however, is the fact that many of their centres have remained important to the present day, including the modern capitals of London, Paris and Bonn.

Below right: the trappings of sophisticated urban life were established early in the southern parts of Gaul—the temple of Augustus and Livia at Vienne was built in the early 1st century AD.

Far right: the foundations of a Celtic temple at Oisseau-le-Petit in northern France. The central temple was surrounded by a temenos, *or sacred enclosure, a plan found throughout northern Gaul and Britain. Celtic gods—often identified with their Roman counterparts—continued to be worshipped in the northern provinces.*

Below: this ceremonial scabbard was found in the Rhine. Richly decorated with gold and silver, it bears the portrait of the Emperor Tiberius (r. AD 14–37). The Rhine legions could make or break emperors, and such gifts to senior officers would have helped to ensure their loyalty.

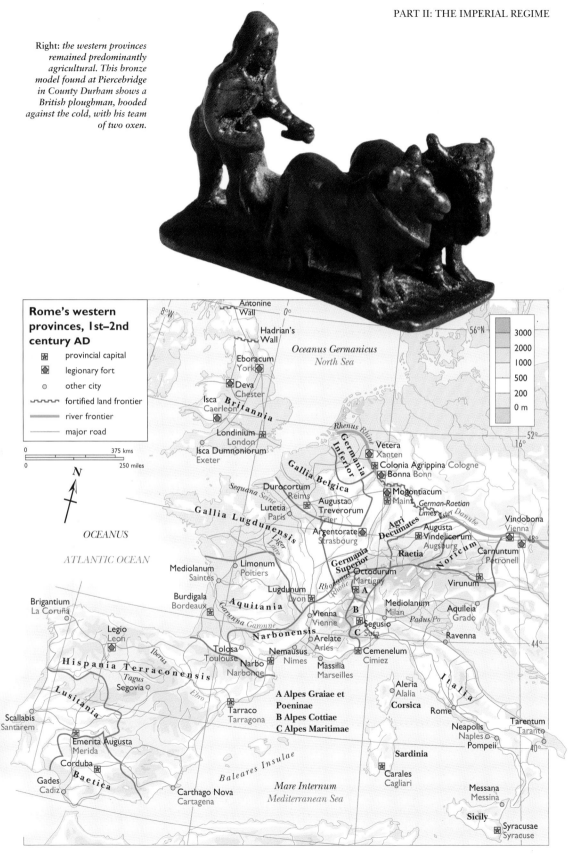

Right: the western provinces remained predominantly agricultural. This bronze model found at Piercebridge in County Durham shows a British ploughman, hooded against the cold, with his team of two oxen.

Rome's western provinces, 1st–2nd century AD

⊠ provincial capital
⊠ legionary fort
○ other city
ⴽⴽⴽⴽ fortified land frontier
━━ river frontier
── major road

0 ———— 375 kms
0 ———— 250 miles

N

Antonine Wall
Hadrian's Wall
Oceanus Germanicus
North Sea

Eboracum York
Deva Chester
Isca Caerleon
Britannia
Londinium London
Isca Dumnoniorum Exeter

Vetera Xanten
Germania Inferior
Colonia Agrippina Cologne
Bonna Bonn
Mogontiacum Mainz
German-Raetian Limes

Gallia Belgica
Durocortum Reims
Lutetia Paris
Augusta Treverorum Trier
Argentorate Strasbourg
Sequana Seine

Gallia Lugdunensis

OCEANUS ATLANTIC OCEAN

Agri Decumates
Augusta Vindelicorum Augsburg
Raetia
Noricum
Vindobona Vienna
Carnuntum Petronell

Germania Superior
Octodurum Martigny
A
Virunum

Mediolanum Saintes
Limonum Poitiers
Lugdunum Lyon
B
Mediolanum Milan
Aquileia Grado
Padus/Po
Ravenna

Brigantium La Coruña
Burdigala Bordeaux
Aquitania
Vienna Vienne
C Segusio Susa
Arelate Arles
Cemenelum Cimiez
Aleria Alalia
Italia
Rome

Legio Leon
Narbonensis
Tolosa Toulouse
Nemausus Nimes
Massilia Marseilles
Corsica

Hispania Terraconensis
Lusitania
Segovia
Tarraco Tarragona

A Alpes Graiae et Poeninae
B Alpes Cottiae
C Alpes Maritimae

Scallabis Santarem
Emerita Augusta Merida
Corduba
Baetica
Gades Cadiz
Carthago Nova Cartagena
Baleares Insulae
Mare Internum Mediterranean Sea
Sardinia
Carales Cagliari
Neapolis Naples
Pompeii
Tarentum Taranto
Messana Messina
Sicily
Syracusae Syracuse

3000 2000 1000 500 200 0 m

55

Three Western Cities

Above: Vesuvius smoulders behind the Temple of Apollo in the main religious enclosure of Pompeii. The Ionic column to the left was set up as a sundial by the duumvirs Sepunius and Errenius.

Pompeii owes its fame to the blanket of ash that rained down from Vesuvius in August 79, entombing the inhabitants, sealing bread in the ovens and election graffiti on the walls, and leaving the most fully pre-served of ancient Roman cities. Since the 18th century, excavations have uncovered large areas and revealed priceless information on city life. There were the customary public buildings: the forum or marketplace, a theatre and gymnasium, and the amphitheatre where gladiatorial displays were held. The sumptuous villas of the wealthy were adorned with peri-style courts and sophisticated wall paintings, while the shops, bars and tav-erns, the bakeries and brothels, show how ordinary people lived.

1 temple of the Genius of Augustus
2 temple of the Lares
3 temple of Fortunae Augustae

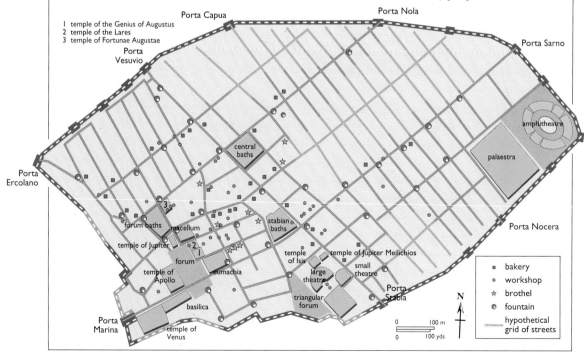

London, founded after the invasion of Britain in AD 43 at an important crossing of the Thames, soon became the capital of the province. In the following decades it was furnished with a forum and basilica, a governor's palace, and (in the early 2nd century) an amphitheatre. The city walls were built in *c.*190, completed by the addition of riverside defences in the late 3rd or early 4th century. London was never one of the great Roman cities, however: new evidence suggests that after a peak in the early 2nd century there was a sharp decline in population, though it remained a centre of government until the collapse of Roman rule in the 5th century.

Above: *this geometrical mosaic floor was discovered in 1869 close to the Mansion House in the City of London. It dates from the 3rd century AD, and its quality and sophistication shows the continuing importance of London in the later Roman period, even though the city was by then in decline as an urban centre.*

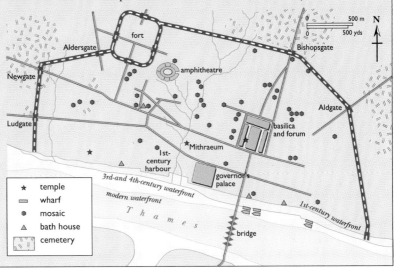

Trier was founded by the Emperor Augustus and developed into the leading city of northeast Gaul. The grid-plan street layout probably dates from the 1st century AD, as does the stone bridge across the Moselle, but the greatest buildings of Roman Trier belong to the 3rd and 4th centuries, when the city rose to prominence as an imperial residence first under the breakaway Gallic emperors (260–74) and then under Constantius and Constantine (293–337). The city walls and the imposing Porta Nigra were probably built during this period. There was also a great imperial palace, with an audience hall (basilica) and a circus or race track, and adjacent to it the enormous Kaiserthermen or Imperial Baths. At its height, the city may have had a population of 80,000.

Left: *the Porta Nigra, the north gate of the Roman city of Trier, was probably built in the 3rd century AD. It owes its survival to the fact that it was later converted into a church and palace for the bishops of Trier.*

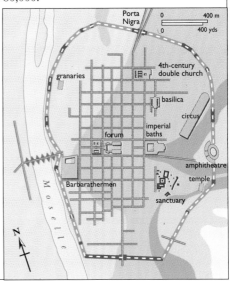

Vespasian and the Jewish War

Roman control of Judaea was resented by religiously-committed Jews, and in the spring of 66 discontent turned into open revolt.

The rebels seized control of Jerusalem, and at Beth-Horon they defeated the force which Cestius Gallus, the Roman governor of Syria, led against them. This success allowed the rebels to seize control of large areas of Judaea and Galilee. Realizing that a determined campaign was now needed to suppress the revolt, the Emperor Nero despatched an experienced military commander, Titus Flavius Vespasianus (Vespasian), with a force of three legions and numerous auxiliaries. In 67 Vespasian recovered Galilee and restored control over the coastal cities of Judaea, and the following year captured Jericho and Emmaus, leaving Jerusalem increasingly isolated.

Vespasian was preparing for the final assault when news came that Nero had been overthrown. Military operations were largely suspended while the situation at Rome was unclear. Then, in July 69, Vespasian himself was proclaimed emperor by the eastern legions, and a few months later he departed for Alexandria and then Rome, leaving the completion of the Jewish War to his son Titus. In September 70, after a seven-month siege, Titus captured Jerusalem. The rebel cause was now hopeless, but groups continued to hold out in the fortresses of Herodium, Machaerus and Masada, until they too were taken by the Romans.

Right: the last action in the war was the siege of Masada in spring 74. The Roman commander Flavius Silva erected an encircling wall with attached forts. He eventually captured the rocky citadel only by building a great siege ramp on a natural spur against its western face, at which point the defenders committed suicide rather than fall into Roman hands.

Right: *this relief, from the arch set up at Rome to commemorate Titus's victory, shows the Temple treasures being carried off by the Romans.*

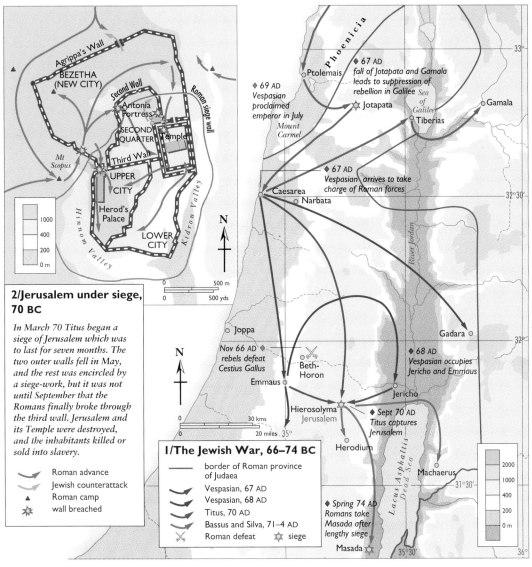

2/Jerusalem under siege, 70 BC

In March 70 Titus began a siege of Jerusalem which was to last for seven months. The two outer walls fell in May, and the rest was encircled by a siege-work, but it was not until September that the Romans finally broke through the third wall. Jerusalem and its Temple were destroyed, and the inhabitants killed or sold into slavery.

Roman advance
Jewish counterattack
▲ Roman camp
✳ wall breached

1/The Jewish War, 66–74 BC

border of Roman province of Judaea
Vespasian, 67 AD
Vespasian, 68 AD
Titus, 70 AD
Bassus and Silva, 71–4 AD
⚔ Roman defeat   ✳ siege

Labels on map 2:
Agrippa's Wall
BEZETHA (NEW CITY)
Second Wall
Antonia Fortress
Roman siege wall
SECOND QUARTER
Temple
Mt Scopus
Third Wall
UPPER CITY
Hinnom Valley
Kidron Valley
Herod's Palace
LOWER CITY
1000 / 400 / 200 / 0 m
0   500 m
0   500 yds
N

Labels on map 1:
Phoenicia
Ptolemais
◆ 67 AD fall of Jotapata and Gamala leads to suppression of rebellion in Galilee
Sea of Galilee
◆ 69 AD Vespasian proclaimed emperor in July
✳ Jotapata
○ Gamala
○ Tiberias
Mount Carmel
◆ 67 AD Vespasian arrives to take charge of Roman forces
Caesarea
○ Narbata
River Jordan
○ Joppa
Nov 66 AD ◆ rebels defeat Cestius Gallus
⚔ Beth-Horon
Emmaus ○
◆ 68 AD Vespasian occupies Jericho and Emmaus
○ Gadara
○ Jericho
Hierosolyma Jerusalem
◆ Sept 70 AD Titus captures Jerusalem
Herodium ○
◆ Spring 74 AD Romans take Masada after lengthy siege
○ Machaerus
Lacus Asphaltis Dead Sea
Masada ✳
2000 / 1000 / 400 / 200 / 0 m
33°
32°30'
32°
31°30'
35° 35°30' 36°
0 30 kms
0 20 miles
N

Trajan's Wars

The Emperor Trajan (98–117) was the first Roman ruler for several decades to conquer new territories and establish new provinces of the empire.

His two great wars were fought against the Dacians and the Parthians. The Dacian kingdom lay north of the Danube in the area of modern Romania. Under its powerful king Decebalus, Dacia had become a threat to Roman supremacy and had defeated Roman armies during the reign of Domitian (81–96). Trajan determined to put an end to this situation by forcing Dacia into submission. During the first Dacian War (101–102), Trajan defeated the Dacians in heavy fighting, and Decebalus came to terms. When he broke these in 105, Trajan embarked on a second campaign aimed at nothing less than the conquest of the whole kingdom, which became the Roman province of Dacia.

By 114 the emperor was back on campaign, fighting against Rome's great eastern rivals the Parthians. That year he conquered the mountain kingdom of Armenia, and the following turned northern Mesopotamia into another Roman province. His most dramatic success came in 116, when his army occupied southern Mesopotamia and advanced as far as the Persian Gulf. The new conquests could not be held, however, and Trajan had already been forced to abandon southern Mesopotamia when he died in August 117.

Right: a relief carving of Roman standard bearers, from the monument set up at Tropeum Traiani (modern Adamclisi) by Trajan to commemorate his successful Dacian campaigns.

Above: The Dacian War brought Trajan enormous wealth from spoils and the sale of slaves. He used this to build a great forum and market at Rome, which were dedicated in 112. The Senate added the monument known as Trajan's Column (above). Carved with a spiral frieze showing episodes from the war, it serves as a memorial to the campaigns and a valuable record of the equipment and appearance of the Roman army in Trajan's day.

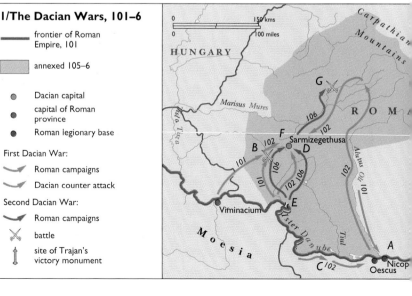

1/The Dacian Wars, 101–6

— frontier of Roman Empire, 101

▨ annexed 105–6

● Dacian capital
● capital of Roman province
● Roman legionary base

First Dacian War:
➤ Roman campaigns
➤ Dacian counter attack

Second Dacian War:
➤ Roman campaigns
✗ battle
⚑ site of Trajan's victory monument

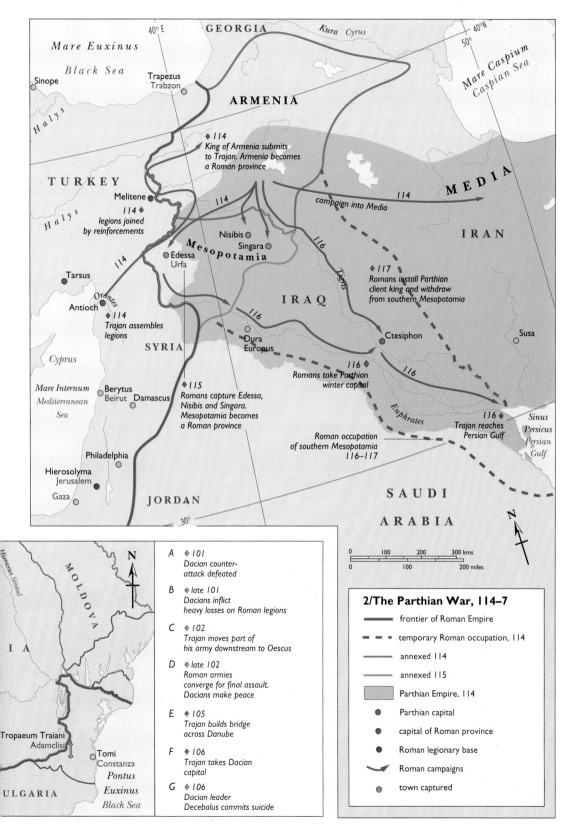

40° E   GEORGIA   *Kura Cyrus*   40°N
50°

Mare Euxinus
Black Sea   *Mare Caspium*
Sinope   *Caspium Sea*
Trapezus
Trabzon
ARMENIA

♦114
King of Armenia submits
to Trajan. Armenia becomes
a Roman province

TURKEY
Melitene   114   *campaign into Media*   114   MEDIA
114 ♦
legions joined
by reinforcements
Halys   IRAN
Nisibis
Mesopotamia Singara   116
Edessa   ♦117
Tarsus   Urfa   Romans install Parthian
                                            client king and withdraw
Orontes   IRAQ   from southern Mesopotamia
Antioch   116
♦114   Susa
Trajan assembles   116
legions   SYRIA   Dura   Ctesiphon
               Europus
Cyprus

Mare Internum Berytus   116 ♦
Mediterranean Beirut Damascus Romans take Parthian
Sea   winter capital   116
♦115   *Euphrates*   116 ♦   *Sinus*
Romans capture Edessa,   Trajan reaches *Persicus*
Nisibis and Singara.   Persian Gulf   *Persian*
Mesopotamia becomes   Roman occupation   *Gulf*
a Roman province   of southern Mesopotamia
Philadelphia   116–117

Hierosolyma
Jerusalem
Gaza   SAUDI
JORDAN   ARABIA   N

30°
                              0   100   200   300 kms
                              0   100   200 miles

Hierasus Siretul   MOLDOVA   N

I A

A ♦101
Dacian counter-
attack defeated

B ♦late 101
Dacians inflict
heavy losses on Roman legions

C ♦102
Trajan moves part of
his army downstream to Oescus

D ♦late 102
Roman armies
converge for final assault.
Dacians make peace

Tropaeum Traiani
Adamclisi

E ♦105
Trajan builds bridge
across Danube
Tomi
Constanza
Pontus   *F* ♦106
Euxinus   Trajan takes Dacian
Black Sea   capital

ULGARIA   *G* ♦106
                Dacian leader
                Decebalus commits suicide

2/The Parthian War, 114–7

——— frontier of Roman Empire

- - - temporary Roman occupation, 114

——— annexed 114

——— annexed 115

▨ Parthian Empire, 114

● Parthian capital

● capital of Roman province

● Roman legionary base

↶ Roman campaigns

● town captured

The Roman Army

Rome grew to greatness on the strength of its army, a disciplined fighting force that proved superior to all its opponents.

From the last centuries BC and throughout the early imperial era, the backbone of the army was the legions, infantry units of around 5000 men, all highly trained and well equipped. Each legion was divided into centuries commanded by junior officers or centurions. Six centuries made up a cohort, and ten cohorts a legion. Legionaries fought mainly with short sword and throwing javelin, protected by a rectangular shield and body-armour. The real strength of the legion lay in its professionalism and discipline, which enabled it to carry out complex manoeuvres in the heat of battle. Legionaries were also responsible for building roads, forts and bridges, and were adept at siege warfare as well as set-piece battles.

Alongside the legionaries were the all-important auxiliaries, non-Roman soldiers recruited from the native peoples of the empire. These operated in cohorts of 500 or 1000 men under the command of a Roman officer, some of them specialist units (such as Syrian archers) fighting with their own preferred weapons. Auxiliaries served for a longer period and were less well paid than legionaries, but on discharge were granted Roman citizenship.

The legions, on the other hand, were recruited only from Roman citizens. In the early Republic they had been taken from landed citizens and peasant farmers with sufficient property to afford to provide their own equipment. Marius changed all that in the late 2nd century BC, allowing landless citizens (including the growing urban proletariat) to enlist. In 31 BC, at the end of the civil wars, a huge force of 60 Roman legions was under arms. Augustus reduced these to 28, stationing them along the frontiers where they were most needed. That still left a Roman army of around 300,000 men, half legionaries and half auxiliaries, representing a huge ongoing commitment in terms of public expenditure.

Above: modern replicas of the weaponry of the Roman legionary: the gladius or short sword, a stabbing weapon which could be used effectively in close combat; the pilum, a heavy javelin with a point designed to bend on impact so that it could not be re-used by the enemy; the shield (scutum), and helmet.

Right: a modern reconstruction of a Roman carro-ballista. The vertical chambers at the front contained the coils used to tension the bow, which could propel a foot-long (30-cm) bolt to a distance of 1000 feet (300 m). A similiar weapon is depicted on the frieze of Trajan's Column.

Under the early empire, legionaries were paid 900 sesterces a year, and signed up for a period of 20 years. They were forbidden to marry during their service, though many did of course form lasting relationships, and their illegitimate children could by the 2nd century win citizenship themselves by joining up as their fathers had done. Domitian raised soldier's pay in the late 1st century, and Septimius Severus again a century later. Severus also allowed legionaries to marry and to live with their families outside the camp. Such concessions may have strengthened the soldiers' loyalty or simply recognized existing reality; but they made the Roman army less mobile and flexible.

During the course of the 3rd and 4th centuries the army was reformed to counter new enemies and changing strategies. Up to this time, forces had been thinly spread along the frontiers, leaving no reserve army for emergencies or special campaigns. The army had also been dominated by the legions of infantry. In the mid-3rd century this was

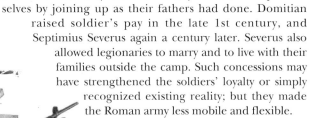

changed by the establishment of a mobile cavalry force, and under Constantine the army was formally divided into frontier troops (or *limitanei*) and a field army (*comitatenses*) both consisting of cavalry and infantry. The field army continued to be a powerful and professional force throughout the 4th century and into the 5th, though increasingly composed of Germanic mercenaries rather than citizen recruits.

Above: *one of the best sources of evidence for the Roman army in action is the spiral relief on Trajan's Column at Rome, commemorating the Dacian Wars of 101–6. The lowest section shows supplies being loaded onto river boats; above this, a boar, a ram and a bull are led to sacrifice while a messenger falls from his horse as Trajan watches from a rostrum; and on the next level, the soldiers build a camp while a Dacian prisoner, possibly a spy, is dragged before the emperor.*

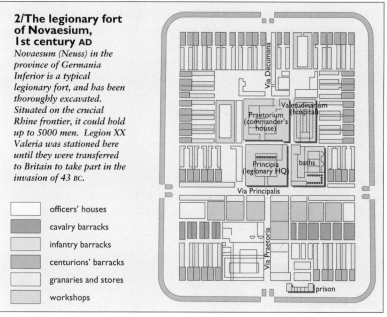

2/The legionary fort of Novaesium, 1st century AD

Novaesum (Neuss) in the province of Germania Inferior is a typical legionary fort, and has been thoroughly excavated. Situated on the crucial Rhine frontier, it could hold up to 5000 men. Legion XX Valeria was stationed here until they were transferred to Britain to take part in the invasion of 43 BC.

- officers' houses
- cavalry barracks
- infantry barracks
- centurions' barracks
- granaries and stores
- workshops

Via Decumana · Valetudinarium (hospital) · Praetorium (commander's house) · Principia (legionary HQ) · baths · Via Principalis · Via Praetoria · prison

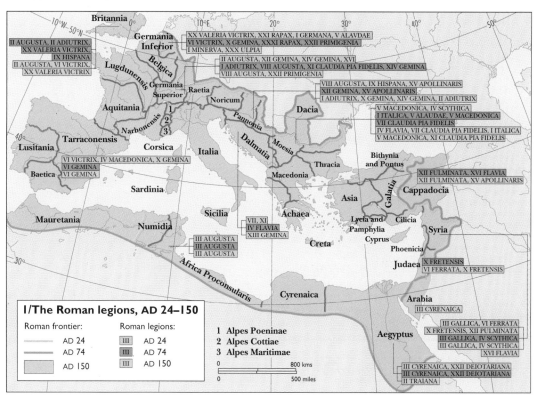

1/The Roman legions, AD 24–150

Roman frontier:
AD 24
AD 74
AD 150

Roman legions:
III AD 24
III AD 74
III AD 150

1 Alpes Poeninae
2 Alpes Cottiae
3 Alpes Maritimae

0   800 kms
0   500 miles

III: The Imperial Peace

The 2nd century was a period of relative stability in the history of the Roman Empire. Trajan's wars carried Roman rule across the Danube into Dacia and southeast into Arabia and Mesopotamia. Under Hadrian, some of the eastern gains were given up, but this still left an empire greater in territorial terms than it had ever been before. Secure within its borders, the Roman state flourished in relative peace and prosperity. Yet this was no happy commonwealth. Despite the pageantry of the monuments and the paternalism of the emperors it remained a world of harsh class divisions, with slaves, peasant farmers and the urban poor eking out a meagre living alongside senators and the rich.

The Frontiers Consolidated

The history of Rome in the 2nd century is much more than that of of individual emperors and their policies, yet there are significant changes from reign to reign which reflect the responses of central government to new problems and circumstances, and some of these bear the stamp of individual rulers. Trajan had been a keen military man, and however much the conquest of Dacia was a strategic necessity, the eastern campaigns at the end of his reign clearly were not. Hadrian sensibly reined back the military machine and set his sights on consolidation rather than conquest. This was shown most clearly by the construction of linear barriers on certain frontiers. The most famous of them are Hadrian's Wall in northern Britain and the German frontier between the Rhine and the Danube. Both were enormous undertakings. The German frontier work consisted of a substantial timber palisade running for almost 350 miles (550 km). Hadrian's British frontier, though much shorter in length—a mere 75 miles (120 km)—made up for this in its even greater solidity: a stone-built structure up to ten feet wide at the base and originally 12 feet (4 m) high, at least in its eastern two thirds—the western section was initially built of turf and only later reinforced with stone.

Opposite: the Pantheon, a temple to all the gods, was founded by Augustus's trusted friend Agrippa in 27 BC. Hadrian entirely remodelled it, retaining Agrippa's porch but replacing the original rectangular structure behind by a daring circular building with an enormous dome even larger in diameter than that of St Peter's in the Vatican. It provides ample proof of Roman mastery of new building techniques, especially the use of brick and concrete, and of their new concepts of architectural design. Alone among Roman temples it has retained its stucco and marble veneer to the present day, providing a unique example of the internal appearance of a great Roman building.

Hadrian's consolidation of the frontiers was perhaps good policy, but it marks a transition in the history of the Roman Empire. The great period of expansion was over, and the role of the army and the emperor was no longer to conquer new territory but to defend what they already controlled. This had to some extent been the case since the death of Augustus a century before—he had warned his successor to keep within existing boundaries and not to embark on any risky foreign adventures. Yet piecemeal expansion had continued, culminating in Trajan's wars of the early 2nd century. Hadrian's frontier policy marked the rejection of further territorial expansion, and gave it physical expression in structures of timber and stone. The army became more and more a defensive force, there to repel foreign invaders and put down rebellions rather than to embark on aggressive wars of conquest. The momentum of expansion was halted, but it was difficult to maintain stability, and as time wore on the Roman empire found itself increasingly fighting a rearguard action against pressures from without. This pressure would ultimately lead to the fall of the Roman Empire in the west.

Above: *the Casa di Diana at Ostia, the port of Rome, was built in the mid-2nd century AD. The ground-floor level was occupied by shops, while stairways lead to apartments on the floors above.*

Government and Rebellion

Hadrian spent much of his 21-year reign travelling around the empire, gaining a level of first-hand experience unrivalled since Augustus. His journeys took him to both eastern and western provinces, and were a mixture of business and pleasure. In the Roman world the centre of government was the emperor and his entourage, wherever they might be, and supplicants or litigants wishing for an audience or commanded to appear before the emperor might find themselves facing a lengthy and expensive voyage. It was only by visiting the provinces themselves, therefore, that an emperor could hope to gain an accurate impression of their problems and needs. Hadrian's travels mark a stage in the gradual transition from an empire of conquered provinces ruled by an Italian aristocracy, to a commonwealth stretching from the Syrian desert to the Atlantic Ocean. It is significant, too, that Hadrian himself, like Trajan before him, was of Spanish extraction although, unlike Trajan, Hadrian was actually born at Rome.

It was on Hadrian's third voyage that he hit upon the scheme that was directly to cause the only major war of his reign. Passing through Palestine, he decided to refound the city of Jerusalem as the colony of Aelia Capitolina, "Aelius" being his family name. Jerusalem and its temple had been destroyed by Titus half a century before, but still held powerful associations for the Jewish community, and the idea of a pagan settlement on their sacred site stirred them into armed rebellion. Led by Simon Bar Cochba, they waged a four-year campaign of open warfare and guerrilla fighting which was serious enough to demand the presence of Hadrian himself.

By the time he returned to Rome in 135 he was a relatively old man, and his final years were devoted to the question of the succession. He himself had been adopted by Trajan, officially on the latter's deathbed (though there were some who claimed that Trajan's widow had manipulated the story and the adoption had never actually taken place). Hadrian too was childless, which once again left him free to name a successor of his choice. He chose Antoninus "Pius", an upright and wealthy Italian nobleman of rather conservative views. As part of the deal Antoninus in turn adopted Marcus Aurelius as his eventual successor. This system of adoption served the Roman Empire well, from Nerva's adoption of Trajan in 97 to Marcus Aurelius's death in 180. It ensured that each new emperor had proved himself capable of government before he assumed power. It removed the vagaries of heredity, which could produce bad emperors as well as good—a point which was brought home when Marcus Aurelius was succeeded not by an adopted emperor but by his own son, the unstable Commodus.

The Antonine Age

The accession of Antoninus Pius in 138 marked the beginning of the Antonine age, a period later looked back to as a kind of golden age in the history of the Roman empire. Antoninus himself reigned for 23 years and was followed by his adopted son, the famous philosopher-emperor Marcus Aurelius. Both were considered estimable rulers in their own rather different ways. Antoninus Pius comes over to us as a benign and paternalistic figure. In sharp contrast with his predecessor Hadrian, he never left Italy once after his accession, and even in earlier life may only have been overseas on one occasion. A number of wars were fought on his orders, but all of them at a distance. The most important was the re-occupation of southern Scotland, which had been abandoned in the time of Domitian. In 159 Antoninus ordered the construction of a new wall, the Antonine Wall, to run between the estuaries of Clyde and Forth. Built of turf and timber rather than stone, it was nonetheless a major undertaking though the area conquered was hardly in itself of world significance. Wars were also fought in Mauretania and along the Danube frontier, but Antoninus was fortunate to face no major crisis and threats alone were sufficient to deter the Parthians, Rome's eastern neighbours, from breaking the peace.

Right: this relief panel depicting the Emperor Marcus Aurelius (161–180) comes from a now-vanished monument, possibly a triumphal arch commemorating his campaigns on the Danube.

Above: the great bronze doors of the Pantheon date from Hadrian's reconstruction of the building in the 2nd century.

While the reign of Antoninus Pius was relatively untroubled, his successor Marcus Aurelius was less fortunate. He assumed power jointly in 161 with his adoptive brother Lucius Verus, but within a year of their accession Verus had had to leave for the east to counter a serious Parthian invasion. In 165 the Romans achieved a major victory, capturing and sacking the Parthian capital of Ctesiphon in southern Mesopotamia. When they returned to Rome the following year, however, they brought back more than just loot—they brought the plague. An epidemic of unspecified nature (though probably not the bubonic plague of Black Death fame) raged throughout the empire in the year 168, carrying off thousands of victims in Rome and other major cities. Perhaps sensing this weakness, Germanic peoples chose this moment to cross the Danube and attack Italy.

This was the start of the Germanic wars which were to preoccupy Marcus Aurelius for the rest of his reign (Lucius Verus dying in 169). They mark, in a sense, the end of Rome's unchallenged greatness, the first time for over 200 years that any foreign people had invaded Italy, and a foretaste of worse things to come. The principal protagonists on this occasion were the Quadi and Marcomanni, Germanic peoples living north of the Danube. Their descent on Italy in 170 created a crisis which took several years to settle. At length order was restored, but not before large areas of the frontier zone had been devastated. Meanwhile Marcus Aurelius was committing his philosophical thoughts to a notebook, entitled simply "To Himself". It is this that has come down to us as the *Meditations*, presenting a gloomy picture of stoicism in the face of hardship and adversity.

The End of a Dynasty

The last years of Marcus Aurelius were occupied by renewed attempts to conquer central Europe, a project which had been abandoned by Augustus almost 200 years before. Then in 180 he died, and all thoughts of advancing the frontier were shelved. Commodus, the new emperor, quickly showed signs of insecurity and megalomania. Leaving it to powerful officials to carry on the work of government, his regime soon became unpopular for its corruption, a situation which was not helped by the idiosyncratic behaviour of the emperor himself. He displayed a great enthusiasm for gladiatorial spectacles, in which he was not only audience but actually participated, taking the role of a *secutor*, armed with sword and shield, against the *retiarius* with his trident and net. His behaviour may not have been as mad as it is reported to us by the Roman historians, but it alienated the elite and eventually posed a threat even to Commodus's own court officials. He planned to make a grand entry into the amphitheatre on New Year's day 193, dressed (once again) as a gladiator. Instead he fell victim to assassination on the last day of 192, being first poisoned and then strangled in his bed. His death marked the end of the Antonine dynasty.

Imperial Buildings

The 2nd-century emperors were great builders, using the resources of the state on a range of impressive projects. Some of them were for the private enjoyment of the emperors themselves. Hadrian, Antoninus Pius and Commodus all had their preferred country villa, in addition to the official imperial palace on the Palatine at Rome. Greatest of all was Hadrian's palatial residence at Tivoli, a series of massive pavilions set in ornamental gardens and richly decorated with sculptures and carvings. Hadrian was especially keen on Greek art and many of the sculptures were copies of famous Greek masterpieces. Antoninus Pius too had his country villa, at Laurentum on the coast south of Rome. Though much less survives than at Tivoli, this too was set within an extensive estate. Commodus in turn chose to spend much of his time away from Rome, though not far away, at the Villa of the Quintillii on the Via Appia, some 6 miles (10 km) from the city centre.

Roman expansion spread the trappings of Greek civic culture throughout the Mediterranean and beyond. Comedians (right) drew their inspiration from the Greek playwright Menander and his Roman imitators Plautus and Terence. By the time the theatre at Dougga, Tunisia (above) was built in the 2nd century AD, the great age of Roman drama was long dead; the last playwright of any stature had been Seneca (d. AD 65), the tutor of Nero and author of a number of gory tragedies. Audiences preferred mime and farce, and many theatres even staged wild beast fights.

Rome remained the heart of the empire, however, and continued to receive much attention in terms of new public buildings and monuments to imperial glory. Victories abroad were marked by the construction of triumphal arches or commemorative columns. The Arch of Constantine is now known to be largely the work of Hadrian, and Marcus Aurelius followed Trajan's example in erecting a great column with spiralling frieze to commemorate his victories in the northern wars. It was Hadrian, however, who devoted the greatest attention to new building at Rome during this period. He completed the reconstruction of the city centre which had been begun by Domitian, but he is famous above all for the rebuilding of the Pantheon. One further series of imperial buildings at Rome deserves particular mention: the temples of the deified emperors. Trajan, Hadrian, Antoninus Pius and Marcus Aurelius were all deified by the senate after their death (Hadrian only after some opposition from the senate). Each then received the temple owing to a god. Trajan's, completed by Hadrian, was in his Forum. The columns of Hadrian's may still be seen in the side of the Stock Exchange in the Piazza di Pietra at Rome. The temple of Antoninus and Faustina (his empress), remodelled in the 17th century as the church of S Lorenzo in Miranda, still stands in the Forum Romanum, and gives some idea of the immense scale which these monuments to the imperial dynasty assumed.

Imperial building was not confined to Rome or Italy. One of the largest projects of the Antonine period was the great baths built on the seafront at Carthage. Hadrian on his travels round the empire also donated buildings in the places he visited, notably the Library and Forum at his much-beloved Athens. And over and above these civil constructions we must reckon the enormous effort put into military camps and frontier works, such as the walls of Hadrian and Antoninus Pius in Britain.

Literature

The early decades of the 2nd century caught the tail end of the greatest period of Latin literature with the historical writings of Tacitus and the later satires of Juvenal. Only slightly later than these are the famous biographies of the first 12 Caesars by Suetonius, who served as secretary to the Emperor Hadrian until he was dismissed for misconduct. These were almost the last great Latin writers in the classical mould. The later part of the century saw Apuleius's comic novel *The Golden Ass*. An anonymous and enigmatic poem called *Pervigilium Veneris* (The Vigil of Venus) may also belong to this period. But Greek had enjoyed a resurgence and was now the main literary language once again, at the expense of Latin. Marcus Aurelius, though a Roman by birth and upbringing, chose Greek as the most appropriate language in which to write his *Meditations*. The greatest Greek writer of the age, however, was undoubtedly Plutarch, a native of Chaeronea in Greece who wrote essays, dialogues and parallel lives of famous Greeks and Romans.

Roman Society in the 2nd Century

The historian Edward Gibbon began his *Decline and Fall of the Roman Empire* with the words "If a man were called to fix the period in the history of the world during which the condition of the human race was most happy and prosperous, he would, without hesitation, name that which elapsed from the death of Domitian to the accession of Commodus. The vast extent of the Roman Empire was governed by absolute power, under the guidance of virtue and wisdom. The armies were restrained by the firm but gentle hand of four successive emperors whose characters and authority commanded involuntary respect."

There is some truth in this picture. It was in this period, for example, that the state established (and encouraged wealthy private citizens to establish) alimentary schemes, where money was lent to landowners and the interest used by local towns and cities to feed and cloth the children of needy families. The state also stepped in to help cities which had borrowed money to embark on public building projects, and become bankrupt as a result.

Yet the picture of the age is not altogether a rosy one. Outbreaks of epidemic disease in the 160s and after were one unpleasant feature. Another was the beginnings of a division of society into *honestiores* and *humiliores*. Previously all Roman citizens had been equal before the law. The major distinction had been between citizens and non-citizens. With the extension of the Roman franchise, however, new social pressures came into being which called for a division between rich citizens and poor. So during the 2nd century a process was set in train which gradually gave more legal privileges and indemnities to the rich, the *honestiores*, at the expense of the poorer citizens, the *humiliores*. An example is a law of Hadrian specifying punishments for those convicted of moving boundary stones (*i.e.* stealing land). Men of standing were merely to be banished, but the rest were to be sentenced to a beating and two years' hard labour. Still harsher treatment was meted out to marginal groups such as Christians who refused to sacrifice to the traditional gods.

Social changes were coupled with economic decline in some regions of the empire. It is doubtful indeed whether Rome ever really adapted to the concept of a fixed territorial base unsupported by the windfall profits of expansionist wars. The capital itself continued to prosper, buoyed up by its position at the heart of a great empire. Other Italian cities were becoming less prosperous, however, and the centre of gravity was steadily shifting away from Italy towards what had once been the dependent provinces. Gaul, the Rhineland, and Africa, in particular, underwent an economic boom in the 2nd century, at the expense of traditional Italian industries. As the economic geography of the empire changed, so did its politics, with provincials becoming ever more prominent and powerful. This, and the growing pressures on the frontiers, were to be hallmarks of the following century.

Right: *the Emperor Commodus (r. AD 181–192) sought to identify himself with the gods; this portrait bust portrays him as Hercules. In a fit of megalomania he renamed the African grain fleet, which brought vital food supplies to Rome, Commodiana Herculea, and the city of Rome itself Colonia Commodiana.*

Hadrian's Travels

The reign of the emperor Hadrian (117–138) was a time of consolidation and retrenchment for the Roman empire.

Hadrian began his reign by abandoning Trajan's eastern conquests (save for Arabia which had come peacefully under Roman rule in 106). Then in 121 he embarked on the first of a series of journeys which took him to practically every corner of the empire.

One of his major concerns was the security of the frontiers, and to this end he strengthened the defences in several areas, including the all-important Rhine and Danube. Hadrian's most famous frontier work was the construction of the wall in northern England which still bears his name, built to divide the Romanized Britons from the barbarians beyond (▶ *page s86–7*).

Hadrian had a great love of Greek culture and much of his travelling was in Greece and the Hellenized eastern provinces. He spent at least three winters at Athens, endowing the city with a library, forum and arch. Hadrian also visited Egypt, travelling up the Nile as far as Thebes. His last eastern journey was however from military necessity rather than tourism; for his plan to refound Jerusalem (destroyed by Titus in AD 70) as the Roman city of Aelia Capitolina sparked off a serious revolt among the Jews which took four years of fierce fighting to suppress.

"His villa at Tibur was marvellously constructed, and he actually gave to parts of it the names of provinces and places ... Lyceum, Academia, Prytaneum, Canopus, Poecile and Tempe. And in order not to omit anything, he even made a Hades."
Life of Hadrian, from the *Historia Augusta*

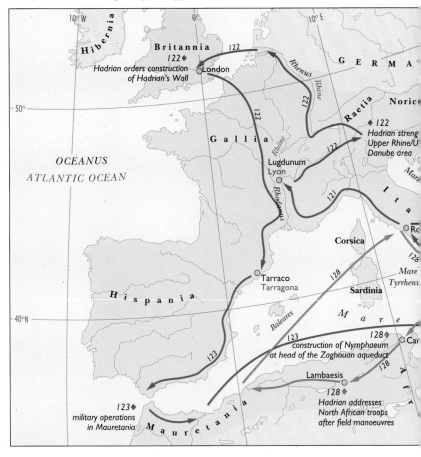

Right: *the legacy of Hadrian's travels may be seen in the palace which he built at Tivoli (Tibur) near Rome. The vast complex of buildings stretched for almost a mile, and incorporated a variety of architectural features inspired by, and named after, places he had visited on his travels. The colonnaded pool named the Canopus was modelled on a famous canal in Egypt, while the Stoa Poecile, or "painted portico", was based on the original at Athens. There was also a theatre (foreground) and a circular pavilion, containing apartments, surrounded by a moat and edged by a semicircular colonnade.*

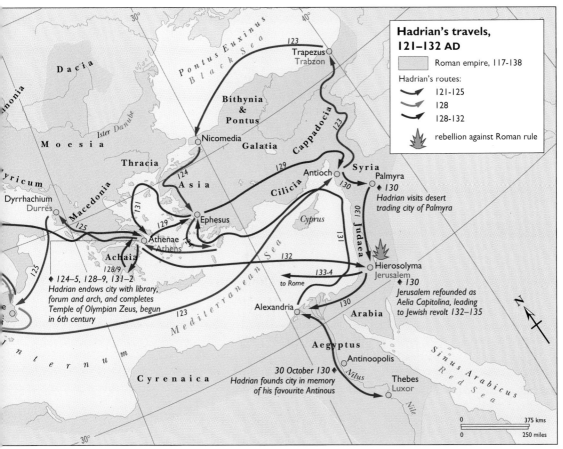

Hadrian's travels, 121–132 AD

Roman empire, 117-138

Hadrian's routes:
- 121-125
- 128
- 128-132

rebellion against Roman rule

Palmyra ◆ 130
Hadrian visits desert trading city of Palmyra

Achaia 128/9 ◆ 124–5, 128–9, 131–2
Hadrian endows city with library, forum and arch, and completes Temple of Olympian Zeus, begun in 6th century

Hierosolyma / Jerusalem ◆ 130
Jerusalem refounded as Aelia Capitolina, leading to Jewish revolt 132–135

Antinoopolis 30 October 130 ◆
Hadrian founds city in memory of his favourite Antinous

The Eastern Provinces

When Rome took control of Asia Minor, the Levant and Egypt in the 1st and 2nd centuries BC, she acquired some of the wealthiest territories of the Mediterranean world.

This was a region where sophisticated urban cultures had been established for centuries. The common language here was Greek rather than Latin, but beneath the Hellenized veneer were a myriad of older local traditions and languages. These included exotic religions such as the cult of many-breasted Artemis at Ephesus, the sun-worship of Heliopolis (Baalbek) and Emesa, and the pharaonic religion of Egypt—not to mention the uncompromising monotheism of the Jews, who were not only to be found in Judaea but also at Alexandria and other centres.

Above: this 5th-century mosaic from Daphne, near Antioch, displays the lively metropolitan life of the Roman east. On the far left a reclining man is served by an attendant. Past the three figures to his right is the Olympic stadium. Beyond it, a man rides up to a bath house. On the far right are the springs for which Daphne was famous.

The Roman peace allowed trade and agriculture to flourish in this multi-ethnic, polyglot world. Buildings and monuments of the early centuries AD bear ample testimony to the prosperity of both individuals and communities. The major cities of Antioch and Alexandria each had populations numbering hundreds of thousands, and even lesser centres such Aphrodisias in Asia Minor or Gerasa (Jerash) in the Levant were embellished with theatres and fountains.

Egypt occupied a special place in the Roman scheme. The fertility given by the annual Nile flood enabled it to produce substantial agricultural surpluses, and grain from Egypt was shipped each year to Rome to feed the urban populace. So important was Egypt within the empire that Augustus forbade any senators from visiting the province without specific permission from the emperor, who ruled it as his personal domain and was worshipped there as a pharoah.

Far right: the temple complex at Philae in southern Egypt, situated on an island in the Nile, was begun under the Ptolemies and completed during the Roman period. The names of Augustus, Caligula and Claudius are recorded in cartouches in the colonnades, and Trajan added a kiosk in the 2nd century. Philae remained a major centre for the worship of Isis and Osiris well into the Christian age, until the cult was suppressed in the 6th century.

Right: the theatre at Bostra was built in the 2nd century AD. This Nabatean city became the capital of the Roman province of Arabia, annexed by Trajan in 106. During the reign of Severus Alexander (222–35) it became a Roman colonia.

The security of the eastern provinces were badly affected by the rise of the powerful Persian empire during the 3rd century AD, but the imperial capital itself was moved from Rome to Constantinople in 330 and the east continued to flourish while the western provinces of Britain, Gaul and Italy itself went into decline. It was only the Islamic invasions of the 7th century which brought an end to Roman hegemony in the region.

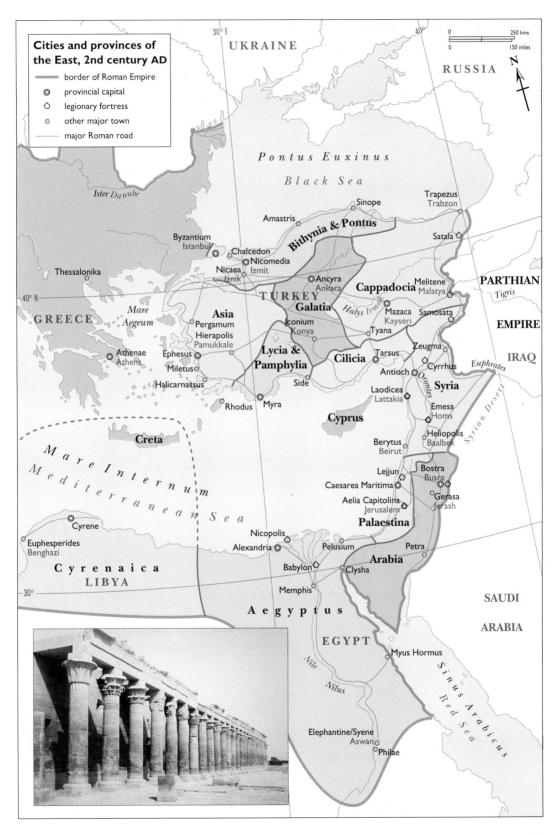

Cities and provinces of the East, 2nd century AD

border of Roman Empire
◎ provincial capital
⬡ legionary fortress
○ other major town
major Roman road

UKRAINE

RUSSIA

N

0   250 kms
0   150 miles

Pontus Euxinus
Black Sea

Ister Danube

Thessalonika

Byzantium
Istanbul
Chalcedon
Nicomedia
Izmit
Nicaea
Iznik

Amastris

Sinope

Trapezus
Trabzon

Satala

Bithynia & Pontus

Ancyra
Ankara

Cappadocia

Melitene
Malatya

PARTHIAN

Galatia

TURKEY

Halys Irmak

Mazaca
Kayseri

Samosata

Tigris

40° N

Mare
Aegeum

Asia
Pergamum
Hierapolis
Pamukkale

GREECE

Iconium
Konya

Tyana

EMPIRE

IRAQ

Lycia &
Pamphylia

Ephesus
Miletus

Athenae
Athens

Halicarnassus

Cilicia

Tarsus

Zeugma

Euphrates

Antioch

Cyrrhus

Orontes

Syria

Side

Rhodus   Myra

Laodicea
Lattakia

Emesa
Homs

Syrian Desert

Cyprus

Heliopolis
Baalbek

Creta

Berytus
Beirut

M a r e   I n t e r n u m
M e d i t e r r a n e a n   S e a

Lejjun

Caesarea Maritima

Bostra
Busra

Gerasa
Jerash

Aelia Capitolina
Jerusalem

Cyrene

Euphesperides
Benghazi

Nicopolis

Alexandria

Pelusium

Palaestina

Petra

Arabia

Babylon   Clysha

C y r e n a i c a
LIBYA

Memphis

30°

SAUDI

ARABIA

A e g y p t u s

EGYPT

Nile

Myus Hormus

Nilus

S i n u s   A r a b i c u s
Red Sea

Elephantine/Syene
Aswan
Philae

75

Three Eastern Cities

Above: one of the most striking remains of Roman Ephesus is the library, built as a memorial to Tiberius Julius Celsus in the early 2nd century AD. Richly adorned with marble columns and facings, it has niches to hold up to 12,000 scrolls; Celsus left a legacy of 25,000 denarii to pay for their purchase.

Ephesus under Roman rule was the leading city of the eastern Aegean and capital of the province of Asia. In the early centuries AD it was extensively rebuilt with colonnaded streets, large bathing complexes and other fine public buildings including a richly decorated library. The life-blood of the city was the thriving port, linked to the sea by a narrow channel and to the city centre by a street edged with colonnades and lit by oil lamps at night. Another source of wealth was the cult of the goddess Artemis, housed in a splendid temple just outside the city and focus of a lively pilgrim trade.

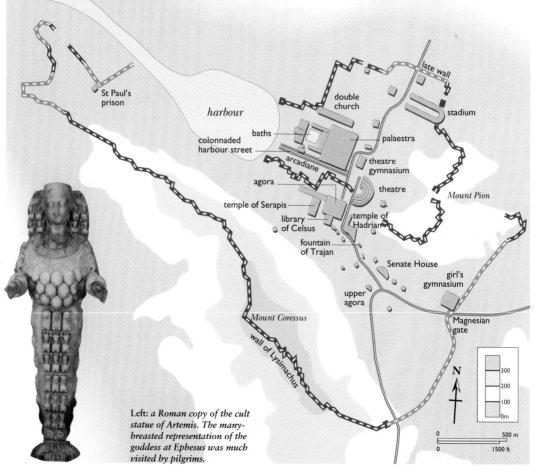

St Paul's prison

harbour

double church

late wall

stadium

baths

palaestra

colonnaded harbour street

arcadiane

theatre gymnasium

agora

theatre

Mount Pion

temple of Serapis

library of Celsus

temple of Hadrian

fountain of Trajan

Senate House

girl's gymnasium

upper agora

Mount Coressus

Magnesian gate

wall of Lysimachus

N

300
200
100
0m

0 — 500 m
0 — 1500 ft

Left: a Roman copy of the cult statue of Artemis. The many-breasted representation of the goddess at Ephesus was much visited by pilgrims.

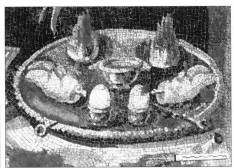

Above: this mosaic of a table setting provides a glimpse of the casual elegance enjoyed by wealthy citizens of Antioch in their palatial villas in the southern suburb of Daphne.

Antioch on the Orontes was the capital of the province of Syria and a city noted for wealth and luxury. Its prosperity derived from trade and from the agricultural produce of the adjacent plain, notably wine and olive oil. Unlike many major Roman cities it was some 15 miles from the sea, but it was connected by a good road to its own harbour town of Seleucia. The city walls are testimony to the fact that from the 3rd century AD Antioch was vulnerable to Persian attack, but it remained an important centre of commerce and government. The sophistication of late Roman Antioch is best illustrated by the luxurious villas of Daphne, a southern suburb noted for its natural beauties.

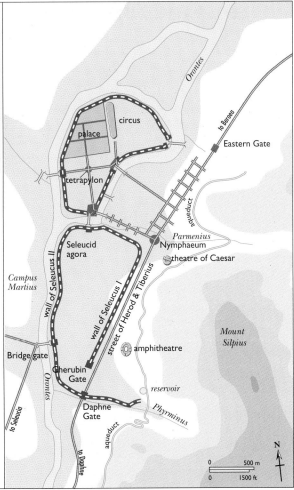

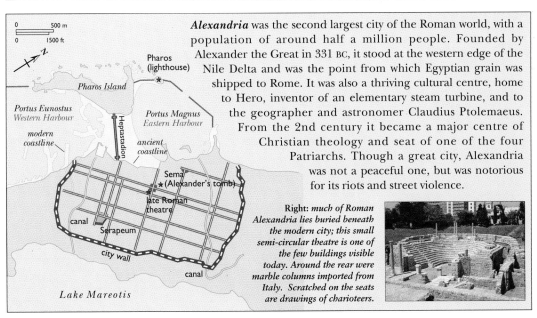

Alexandria was the second largest city of the Roman world, with a population of around half a million people. Founded by Alexander the Great in 331 BC, it stood at the western edge of the Nile Delta and was the point from which Egyptian grain was shipped to Rome. It was also a thriving cultural centre, home to Hero, inventor of an elementary steam turbine, and to the geographer and astronomer Claudius Ptolemaeus. From the 2nd century it became a major centre of Christian theology and seat of one of the four Patriarchs. Though a great city, Alexandria was not a peaceful one, but was notorious for its riots and street violence.

Right: much of Roman Alexandria lies buried beneath the modern city; this small semi-circular theatre is one of the few buildings visible today. Around the rear were marble columns imported from Italy. Scratched on the seats are drawings of charioteers.

Writing and Literacy

Writing was a key feature of Roman society: in monumental inscriptions, literary works, personal letters and bureaucratic records—even as graffiti on the walls.

"Here are my jokes and witticisms, my loves, my sorrows, complaints and vexations; now my style is simple, now more elevated..."
Pliny the Younger, *Letters*

Right: *this wall painting from Pompeii shows a young woman with stylus and set of wooden writing tablets (1st century* AD).

Below right: *among the many wooden writing tablets recovered at the fort of Vindolanda on the northern frontier of Roman Britain was this invitation to a birthday party, written around AD 100:*
"Claudia Severa to her Lepidina, greetings. I send you a warm invitation to come to us of September 11th, for my birthday celebrations, to make the day more enjoyable by your presence. Give my greetings to your Cerialis. My Aelius greets you and your sons. I will expect you, sister. Farewell sister, my dearest soul, as I hope to prosper, and greetings."
Sulpicia Lepidina was the wife of the garrison commander. Her friend's greeting at the end of the letter is the earliest known writing in Latin by a woman.

How many Romans could read or write for themselves is rather a difficult question. The wealthy were taught these skills by a private teacher as part of their childhood education. The less privileged had to rely on other means of learning, persuading a friend or relative to teach them, or (in towns and cities) attending a school. Education was rarely free, but it seems that even among the poor there were some who could read and write. High-flown prose and artful rhetoric may have been the preserve of a small elite, but

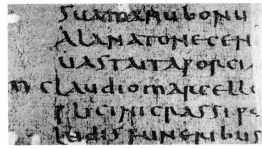

Above: In Roman libraries, the scrolls were stored in pigeonholes; a small parchment label was fixed to the end of each scroll. This engraving was made from a carving found in the 17th century at Neumagen near Trier, but subsequently lost.

Above right: this 3rd-century papyrus from Oxyrhynchus in Egypt preserves an epitome of the Roman historian Livy (59 BC–AD 17). Many ancient works have survived only as epitomes (abridgements). Livy wrote 142 books of history; of these, 35 survive intact, many of the rest as epitomes.

Below: many cities of the highly-literate eastern provinces had fine public libraries. The Emperor Hadrian, an art-lover with a strong interest in Greek culture, had this library built at Athens after his visit in AD 124.

the everyday writing of workmen's accounts or simple letters was relatively widespread, at least among the urban populace, as was the ability to read public posters and inscriptions.

Several different materials were used for written documents. In the east, and even in Italy, papyrus was widely employed. This was made from the pith of an Egyptian marsh plant, pounded in layers to make a form of paper which could then be written on in ink. Several papyrus documents of the Roman period have been preserved in the dry sands of Egypt. They include the oldest surviving gospel fragment, part of St John's gospel, written probably in the 2nd century AD. An alternative to papyrus where that was either unavailable or too expensive was parchment or vellum, made from the skins of cattle, sheep and goats. Wooden stylus tablets, with a recessed surface covered in coloured wax, were another possibility. Here the written message was inscribed in the wax using a bronze or iron stylus. Stylus tablets could be re-used by smoothing out the wax ready to receive a new message (as scratches on the underlying wood often reveal) but were not only for temporary writings but for wills and legal contracts.

Wooden leaf tablets (thin sheets of wood) were also written on in ink. They were so thin that they could be folded, and an address written on the outer face. Alternatively, they could be tied together at the edges in a concertina-like arrangement. Parchment and papyrus documents during the early Roman period (as in classical Greece) were stored mainly in the form of rolls, up to 16 feet (5 m) long, occasionally with rollers at either end. They could be kept in boxes or on shelves, but were clumsy and cumbersome for easy reference. A major innovation (though one which was slow to catch on) was the invention of the book or codex, in which leaves of parchment were bound together down one edge. Books made their first appearance in the 2nd century AD, mainly for Christian texts, but it was not until the 4th century that they came into general use.

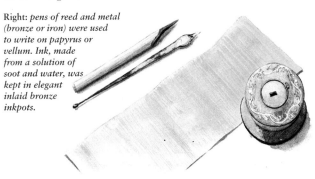

Right: pens of reed and metal (bronze or iron) were used to write on papyrus or vellum. Ink, made from a solution of soot and water, was kept in elegant inlaid bronze inkpots.

Trade and Transport

Efficient road and sea communications allowed goods to be traded throughout the Roman Empire and far beyond its frontiers.

Above: *this bronze coin of Nero (AD 54–68) was issued to commemorate the completion of the harbour of Ostia at the mouth of the River Tiber near Rome. It shows a bird's eye view of the basin surrounded by wharfs and full of shipping. The reclining figure in the foreground represents the Tiber.*

The Romans are famous for the roads they built to connect the far-flung provinces of their empire. These allowed the armies to be deployed rapidly, and helped to stimulate the economy by assisting the transport of goods from town to town. The Romans used both two-wheeled and four-wheeled carts pulled by horses or oxen. There may even have been a rule about keeping to one side of the road, though whether right or left is still disputed. Armies and emperors travelled mainly by road, but for the transport of bulky goods water transport was more efficient: from the Edict of Prices laid down by the Emperor Diocletian in 301 we learn that it was cheaper to ship grain from Spain to Syria than move it 75 miles inland. Large numbers of Roman shipwrecks around the shores of the Mediterranean testify to the scale of maritime trade, as well as its risks. Among the most important commodities were wine, olive oil and grain. Wine and olive oil travelled in large pottery *amphorae* packed in straw, though wine could also be carried in casks. Grain had a particular place in the Roman economy, being shipped from Egypt and Africa (modern Tunisia) to Rome to provide the monthly corn dole for the urban citizenry.

Most inhabitants of the empire survived, as they had always done, on the produce of their local area. The exception was the rich, who used their wealth to purchase exotic luxuries. These included silks from China, incense from Arabia and spices from Southeast Asia. Some of these goods travelled along the so-called Silk Route through Central Asia, others by sea across the Indian Ocean. In exchange, Roman merchants traded gold, glassware and other manufactures, which turn up today as far afield as Malaysia and Vietnam.

Below: *this stretch of Roman road at Vulci, Italy, still survives in remarkably good repair. These essential arteries of communication were solidly constructed to withstand the elements and provide an all-weather surface.*

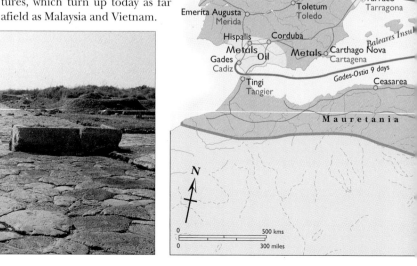

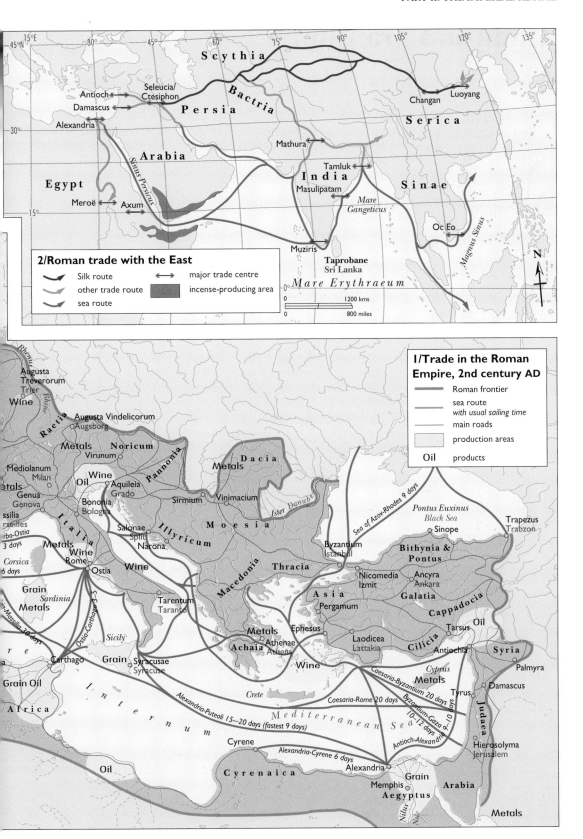

2/Roman trade with the East

- ⟶ Silk route
- ⟶ other trade route
- ⟶ sea route
- ⟷ major trade centre
- ▓ incense-producing area

0 — 1200 kms
0 — 800 miles

Scythia
Bactria
Persia
Serica
Antioch
Seleucia/Ctesiphon
Damascus
Alexandria
Arabia
Egypt
Meroë ⟷ Axum
Sinus Persicus
Mathura
India
Masulipatam
Mare Gangeticus
Tamluk
Sinae
Changan
Luoyang
Oc Eo
Magnus Sinus
Muziris
Taprobane
Sri Lanka
Mare Erythraeum

N

1/Trade in the Roman Empire, 2nd century AD

- Roman frontier
- sea route *with usual sailing time*
- main roads
- production areas
- Oil products

Rhenus Rhine
Augusta Treverorum Trier
Wine
Raetia
Augusta Vindelicorum Augsburg
Metals
Noricum
Virunum
Mediolanum Milan
Wine
Oil
etals
Genua Genova
Aquileia Grado
Bononia Bologna
Italia
ssilia
rseilles
rbo-Ostia
3 days
Metals
Wine
Rome
Ostia
Corsica
6 days
Grain
Sardinia
Metals
Sicily
Carthago
Africa
Grain Oil
Grain
Syracusae
Syracuse
Pannonia
Sirmium
Vinimacium
Dacia
Metals
Ister Danube
Moesia
Illyricum
Salonae
Split
Narona
Wine
Tarentum
Taranto
Macedonia
Thracia
Byzantium
Istanbul
Sea of Azov-Rhodes 9 days
Pontus Euxinus
Black Sea
Sinope
Trapezus
Trabzon
Bithynia & Pontus
Nicomedia
Izmit
Ancyra
Ankara
Asia
Pergamum
Galatia
Cappadocia
Ephesus
Metals
Athenae
Athens
Achaia
Wine
Laodicea
Lattakia
Cilicia
Tarsus
Oil
Antiochia
Syria
Palmyra
Cyprus
Metals
Tyrus
Damascus
Caesaria-Byzantium 20 days
Caesaria-Rome 20 days
Byzantium-Gaza 20 days
Crete
Inter num
Mediterranean Sea
Alexandria-Puteoli 15–20 days (fastest 9 days)
Alexandria-Cyrene 6 days
Antioch-Alexandria
Byzantium-Gaza 10-12 days
Cyrene
Cyrenaica
Oil
Memphis
Alexandria
Grain
Aegyptus
Arabia
Nilus Nile
Judaea
Hierosolyma
Jerusalem
Metals

The Roman Amphitheatre

The Roman passion for gladiatorial games led to the construction of vast amphitheatres. Their impressive ruins can still be seen across Europe and North Africa.

"I chanced to stop in at a midday show, expecting fun, wit, and some relaxation... It was just the reverse... in the morning men are thrown to the lions and the bears, at noon they are thrown to their spectators... 'Kill him! Lash him! Burn him!...' And when the show stops for intermission, 'Let's have men killed meanwhile! Let's not have nothing going on!'"

Seneca, *Moral Epistles*

The games played a major part in Roman life, especially in Italy and the western provinces, where they were the scene for frequent and often bloody displays. The most familiar are the contests between gladiators, trained fighters not unlike the boxers of today, but armed in much deadlier fashion with net and trident (the *retiarius*) or sword, shield and helmet (the *secutor*). These were the classic combatants, but there were other kinds of gladiator, often heavily armoured. Not all those taking part were trained or prepared. Criminals condemned to death—including Christians on occasion—were sometimes compelled to fight each other or exposed naked to wild animals in the arena. Thousands of animals perished in these spectacles—as many as 11,000 in the great games held by Trajan in 107. Most elaborate of all were the sea-fights, fought (if we may believe it) in flooded amphitheatres or on special lakes built for the purpose.

The violence of Roman games has troubled many modern—and some ancient—commentators, but it does not mean that the Roman spectators were any more bloodthirsty than modern viewers of violent films and television series. This was violence at a distance, in a carefully controlled context. Gladiatorial combats were eventually banned by the Emperor Honorius (395–423), but the tradition of the Roman games lives on in the bullfights of Spain and Southern France.

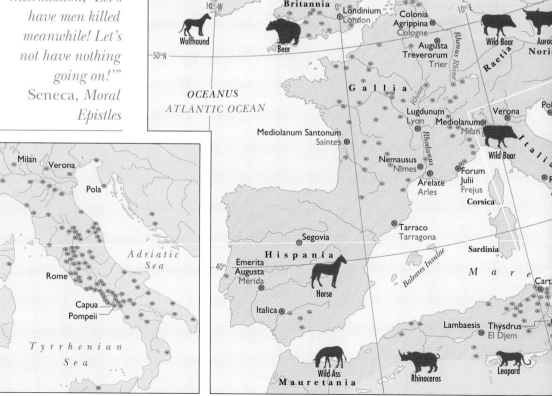

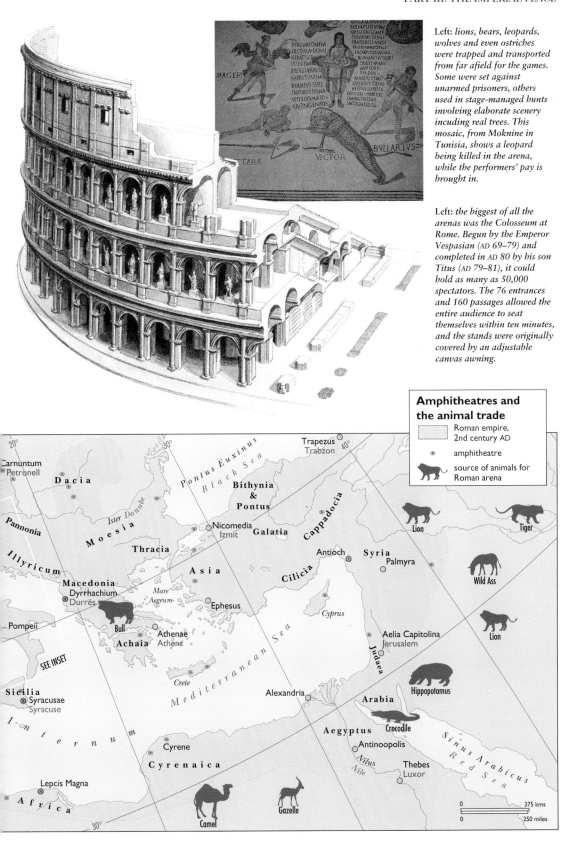

Left: *lions, bears, leopards, wolves and even ostriches were trapped and transported from far afield for the games. Some were set against unarmed prisoners, others used in stage-managed hunts involving elaborate scenery incuding real trees. This mosaic, from Moknine in Tunisia, shows a leopard being killed in the arena, while the performers' pay is brought in.*

Left: *the biggest of all the arenas was the Colosseum at Rome. Begun by the Emperor Vespasian (AD 69–79) and completed in AD 80 by his son Titus (AD 79–81), it could hold as many as 50,000 spectators. The 76 entrances and 160 passages allowed the entire audience to seat themselves within ten minutes, and the stands were originally covered by an adjustable canvas awning.*

Amphitheatres and the animal trade

Roman empire, 2nd century AD

⊛ amphitheatre

source of animals for Roman arena

Roman Spain

The Iberian peninsula was one of the most prosperous regions of the Roman Empire, with great cities and a thriving export trade.

The peninsula was divided into three separate provinces: Lusitania in the west, Baetica in the south, and Tarraconensis in the east and north. The Roman conquest was a long drawn-out affair, beginning in 206 BC with the capture of Carthaginian possessions in the south (▶ *pages 24–5*) and ending with the crushing of the last resistance in the northwest in 19 BC. By this time, the southern region of Spain was thoroughly Romanized. A network of roads connected its towns and cities, crossing the major rivers on fine stone bridges such as the one that spans the Tagus at Alcantara. Several Iberian cities, including Emerita Augusta (Mérida), Corduba (Cordoba), Hispalis (Seville) and Carthago Novo (Cartagena), were substantial places with all the trappings of urbanized Roman life; at Mérida, the 2nd-century theatre, with its impressive porticoed stage-front (*scaenae frons*), survives and is still used for theatrical productions.

Above: pottery containers (amphorae) for transporting Spanish wine, olive oil and fish sauce have been found all around the shores of the western Mediterranean. They form one of the main components of the rubbish mounds behind the waterfront at Rome and some, with manufacturers' marks from Spain, have been found as far afield as Wroxeter in Britain and Heddernheim in Germany.

At the end of the 1st century, Spain provided the first Roman emperor of provincial origin in the person of Trajan (*r.* 98–117), born probably at Italica near modern Seville. Trajan's successor Hadrian (*r.* 117–138) was also of Spanish origin. Families such as those of Trajan and Hadrian drew much of their wealth from the agricultural produce of southern Spain, particularly from the export of wine and olive oil. Spain was also an exporter of the highly-prized fish sauce known as *garum*, which was processed in factories along the southern coast. The most obviously profitable of Roman Spain's resources, however, were its metals: gold in the northwest, copper and silver in the southwest. In the Rio Tinto area remains of the screw pumps and water wheels used to drain the deep workings still survive, providing vivid evidence of Roman hydraulic capabilities (▶ *pages 128–9*).

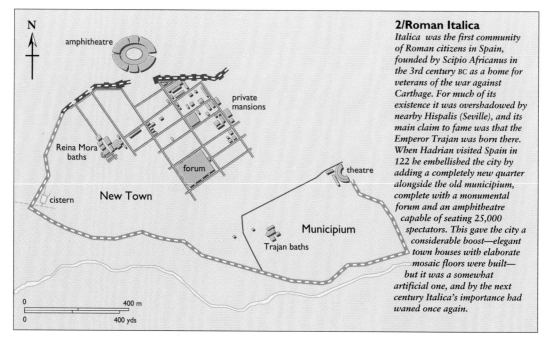

2/Roman Italica

Italica was the first community of Roman citizens in Spain, founded by Scipio Africanus in the 3rd century BC as a home for veterans of the war against Carthage. For much of its existence it was overshadowed by nearby Hispalis (Seville), and its main claim to fame was that the Emperor Trajan was born there. When Hadrian visited Spain in 122 he embellished the city by adding a completely new quarter alongside the old municipium, complete with a monumental forum and an amphitheatre capable of seating 25,000 spectators. This gave the city a considerable boost—elegant town houses with elaborate mosaic floors were built—but it was a somewhat artificial one, and by the next century Italica's importance had waned once again.

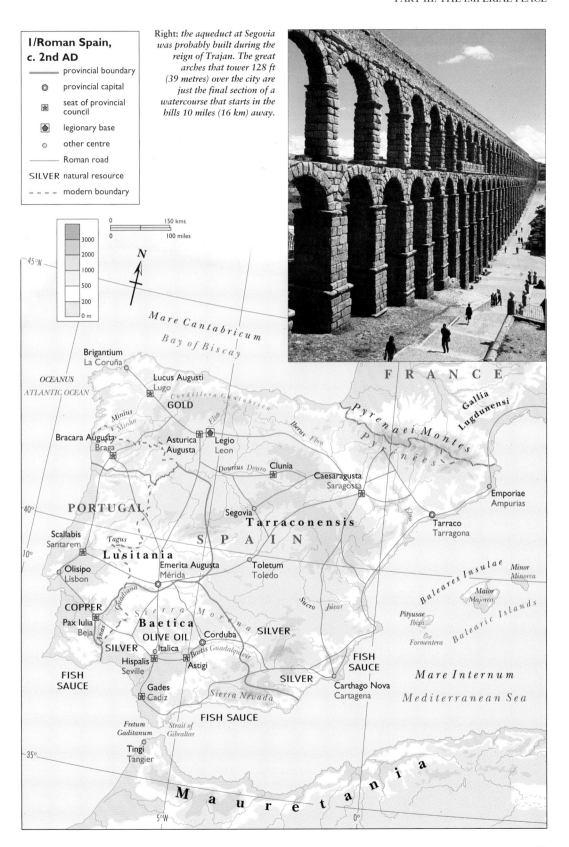

I/Roman Spain, c. 2nd AD

─────	provincial boundary
◎	provincial capital
⊞	seat of provincial council
◈	legionary base
○	other centre
─────	Roman road
SILVER	natural resource
- - - -	modern boundary

Right: the aqueduct at Segovia was probably built during the reign of Trajan. The great arches that tower 128 ft (39 metres) over the city are just the final section of a watercourse that starts in the hills 10 miles (16 km) away.

3000
2000
1000
500
200
0 m

0   150 kms
0   100 miles

N

45°N

Mare Cantabricum
Bay of Biscay

OCEANUS
ATLANTIC OCEAN

Brigantium
La Coruña

Lucus Augusti
Lugo

Cordillera Cantabrica

GOLD

Minius Minho

Bracara Augusta
Braga

Asturica
Augusta

Elsa

Legio
Leon

Dourius Douro

Clunia

Caesaragusta
Saragossa

Iberus Ebro

Pyrenaei Montes
Pyrénées

Gallia
Lugdunensi

F R A N C E

Emporiae
Ampurias

Ebro

40°

PORTUGAL

Segovia

Tarraconensis

Tarraco
Tarragona

Scallabis
Santarem

Tagus

Lusitania

S P A I N

Olisipo
Lisbon

Emerita Augusta
Mérida

Toletum
Toledo

10°

Baleares Insulae

Minor
Minorca

Maior
Majorca

Sucro Jucar

COPPER

Pax Iulia
Beja

Sierra Morena

Baetica

OLIVE OIL

Corduba

SILVER

Pityusae Ibiza

Formentera

Balearic Islands

SILVER

Italica

Baetis Guadalquivir

Hispalis
Seville

Astigi

Anas
Guadiana

FISH
SAUCE

SILVER

FISH
SAUCE

Gades
Cadiz

Sierra Nevada

SILVER

Carthago Nova
Cartagena

Mare Internum
Mediterranean Sea

FISH SAUCE

Fretum Gaditanum

Strait of Gibraltar

Tingi
Tangier

35°

M a u r e t a n i a

5°W

0°

Guarding the Frontiers

The peace and prosperity of the empire depended on the defence of its frontiers, which were guarded by forts, watchtowers and ramparts.

Until the middle decades of the 3rd century, Rome had no mobile field army held in reserve, and military units were concentrated in camps and forts along the frontiers. It was the defence of these frontiers which gave the provinces the security which allowed their economies to flourish and provide taxes for the imperial treasury. Not surprisingly, then, maintaining and strengthening the frontiers was a major preoccupation of government. At first this was achieved by building a chain of forts and watch-towers linked by a military road to allow the rapid deployment of troops. Under Hadrian (117–38), however, crucial sections of the frontier began to be fortified in more substantial manner by the building of a continuous rampart or wall. The most famous and elaborate is Hadrian's Wall, the 70-mile (112-km) stone wall running from the mouth of the River Tyne to the Solway Estuary, and extended down the Cumbrian coast by forts and watchtowers. In its central section Hadrian's Wall runs across rugged terrain, and substantial stretches of the wall and its forts, milecastles and turrets can still be seen.

On the European mainland there was generally no need for such a continuous barrier, since

Above: *a stretch of Hadrian's wall. In the foreground is a turret, which would have been used for observation and defence. The wooden superstructure is based on the turrets depicted on Trajan's Column at Rome. In the distance is a milecastle, a more substantial defence with barrack accommodation. There were two turrets between each milecastle.*

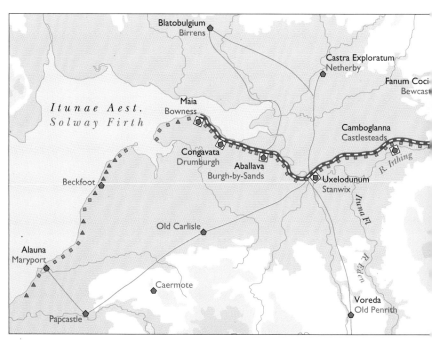

the frontier ran along the Rhine and the Danube, which themselves formed a sufficient obstacle. Forts, camps and watchtowers were built along their banks, and a strong frontier-work was constructed between the upper reaches of the two rivers. New frontier defences continued to be built during the late Roman period, especially along the Danube where pressure from the north was intense. These include a series of boundary earthworks, the Devil's Dykes and Brazda lui Novac du Nord, built by Constantine (306–37) to protect tributary peoples beyond the Danube from the Goths.

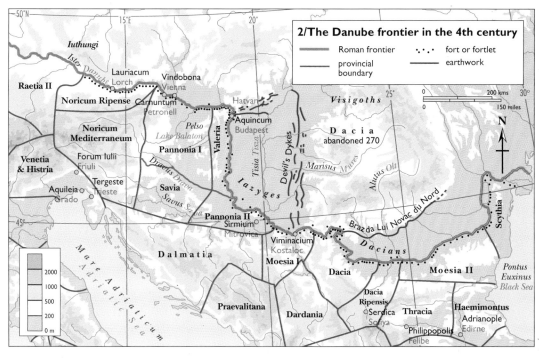

2/The Danube frontier in the 4th century

- Roman frontier
- provincial boundary
- fort or fortlet
- earthwork

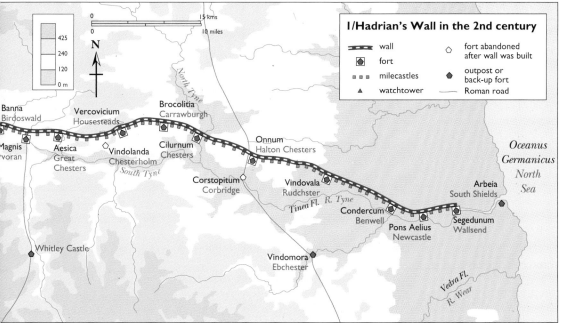

1/Hadrian's Wall in the 2nd century

- wall
- fort
- milecastles
- watchtower
- fort abandoned after wall was built
- outpost or back-up fort
- Roman road

IV: The Troubled Century

The century following the death of Commodus was marked by a remarkable series of shifts in Roman fortunes, greater than the empire had ever experienced before. A period of firm government by the early Severans was followed by a gradual decline of central authority. Coupled with the appearance of more powerful enemies on the imperial frontiers, this led to a crisis in the security and stability of the empire which lasted throughout the middle decades of the 3rd century. Riven by internal faction and assailed by foreign enemies, the empire broke up into a number of regional powers. For a moment it looked as though all was lost, as though the Roman empire was at an end. But a series of capable military emperors managed to restore the position during the course of the 270s, laying the groundwork for the major reorganization undertaken by Diocletian after his accession in 284.

The murder of Commodus on New Year's Eve 192 brought to an end the Antonine age, but while Commodus himself had been unpopular with both the Senate and the praetorian guard, his demise did not at once usher in peace. The assassins, with the support of the Senate, made the elderly Pertinax emperor. He was a respected statesman and distinguished military commander, but he too lacked the support of the praetorians and was murdered by elements of the guard in March 193.

This marks the high point of praetorian fortunes; never again were they to exercise such power at Rome. Their immediate move was to offer the position of emperor to the person who would pay them the most money, and the choice thus fell upon the wealthy but ineffectual Didius Julianus. He had no support in the provinces, and the frontier legions soon began to declare for their own candidates: Pescennius Niger in the east, Clodius Albinus in Britain, Septimius Severus on the Danube. Severus was the eventual winner, largely by being bolder and more ruthless than his competitors. He marched on Rome and easily disposed of Didius Julianus, but had hard fighting to do before he overcame Pescennius Niger and Clodius Albinus. It was not until 197, over four years after Commodus's death, that Severus had undisputed rule over the whole empire.

With one short break, members of the Severan family were to govern Rome for more than 40 years. This marks a further step in the growing importance of the provincials, especially those from the African and eastern provinces. Severus himself was born at Lepcis Magna in Cyrenaica (modern Libya). His rival Clodius Albinus came from Hadrumetum (Sousse) in modern Tunisia. By this time, a large proportion of the senators at Rome were of African origin. Most of them in fact supported Albinus rather than Severus, which caused Severus to instigate a purge of 29 senators once he had defeated Albinus. Severus's African origins were plain for all to hear in his African accent, which he never lost.

To African was mixed a Syrian element, since Severus was married to Julia Domna, daughter of the High Priest of the sun-god Elagabal at Emesa (modern Homs). Thus Caracalla (211–17), Severus's successor, was half African, half Syrian, and he in turn was succeeded after a brief interlude by

Right: the Emperor Septimius Severus (r.193–211), with his wife Julia Domna and their sons Caracalla and Geta. Severus left the empire to his two sons, but in 212 Caracalla murdered his brother. Thousands of Geta's supporters were also killed, his statues smashed and his portraits—including this one—defaced.

his mother's sister's grandchildren Marcus Aurelius (Elagabalus) (218–22) and Alexander Severus (222–35), both of whom were pure Syrian.

The Empire under the Severans

Septimius Severus relied heavily on the support of the army both to bring him to power and to retain it. He naturally paid particular attention to military matters, waging a series of wars, raising new legions and improving the soldiers' pay and conditions for the first time since Domitian a century earlier. Legionaries were now allowed to marry and to live with their wives and families in civilian accommodation outside the military camps.

His major wars against foreign enemies were in Britain and the east. Severus fought two separate campaigns against the Parthians, in 195 and 197–8, and created two new imperial provinces (Mesopotamia and Osrhoene) in the Parthian borderlands beyond the Euphrates. These were the first significant additions to the empire since Trajan's conquest of Dacia some 90 years before. The war in Britain came near the end of the reign, and was nothing less than an attempt to revive the plan of conquering the whole of Scotland. Neither this nor the Parthian wars may be considered to have been a strategic necessity, though they brought booty and glory to the army. One further objective of the British war, we are told, was to remove Severus's troublesome sons from the hothouse politics of Rome.

Another area where Septimius Severus took serious military action was North Africa, his home territory. Lepcis Magna received a suite of impressive new public buildings befitting the birthplace of an emperor. Severus also campaigned against the desert nomads and ordered the construction of a new system of roads and forts which pushed the frontier significantly further to the south. He also created the new province of Numidia. The importance of Africa went well beyond its close links with the imperial family. It continued to be one of the most prosperous provinces of the empire, producing huge quantities of oil from vast olive groves, and continuing to be a major supplier of grain for the city of Rome. The economic success of the African provinces is amply demonstrated by great building projects of the 2nd and early 3rd centuries, such as the amphitheatre at El Djem.

In Italy, on the other hand, the Severan period was characterized by continuing economic decline. Politically, Italians were becoming steadily less important as provincials took more and more of the key positions. The influence of the Senate, too, was falling, as members of the equestrian order (many of them as wealthy as senators, but distinguished from them by being non-political) were given plum commands. The realities of power were reflected by Severus's stationing of one of his three new legions in Italy, as if it were just another province. The legion was based at Albanum, a mere 20 miles from Rome, as a visible proof of the emperor's authority over Senate and capital.

Right: the praetorian guard, shown here in a relief carving from Rome, were the elite bodyguard of the emperors. They reached the height of their power and influence in 193 when, after assassinating the Emperor Pertinax, they put the empire up for sale to the highest bidder.

Rome itself, however, was neither neglected by the Severans nor abandoned as an imperial residence. Quite the contrary. Severus added a new wing to the Palatine palace, a triumphal arch in the Forum, and may have begun construction of the baths named after his son Caracalla. The later Severans also built at Rome, Elagabalus, for instance, erecting an enormous temple on the Palatine to the sun god he worshipped.

Right: Septimius Severus came from Lepcis Magna in Tripolitana, a region then at the zenith of prosperity. The source of this wealth was the agricultural produce of the farming villas and their surrounding estates. This one, at Utica in Byzacena (modern Tunisia), is one of the best-preserved in the Roman world.

The Severan Succession

Septimius Severus died at York in 211 and was followed by his sons Marcus Antoninus (nicknamed Caracalla after his favourite type of cloak) and Geta. The two were constantly at odds with each other, and though each built up a substantial following at Rome, it was Caracalla who eventually won the struggle, having Geta murdered after only a few months of joint rule. Caracalla spent the rest of his reign on a grand tour of the eastern provinces. The notoriety he gained by murdering his brother was reinforced by his unexplained massacre of the young male population of Alexandria when he visited the city in 215. Like his father, he increased the pay of the soldiers, on whom he depended, and like him too he mounted a major war against the Parthians. The first foray, in 216, was an unqualified success, so far as it went, though by early the following year the Parthians had regrouped and were poised for a major counter-offensive. Caracalla did not live to face the threat, since he was murdered by one of his bodyguard, a man with a private grievance, in spring 217.

He left two great monuments to his five-year reign, one physical, the other constitutional. The physical monument was the enormous Baths of Caracalla, the greatest of Roman bathing complexes, which was dedicated

Right: *Dougga, in modern Tunisia, was one of the flourishing Roman cities of North Africa. Its grand public buildings included the capitol—a temple of the Capitoline triad of deities, Jupiter, Juno and Minerva. This was dedicated in AD 166, and the pediment sculpture depicts the apotheosis of the Emperor Antoninus Pius, who had died five years earlier.*

in 216 but further added to during the 220s. The constitutional reform for which he is best known is the granting in 212 of Roman citizenship to all the free male inhabitants of the empire. It was not as radical a move as it seemed. Many provincials already possessed Roman citizenship through grants by earlier emperors. It did remove a major constitutional distinction between Italians and non-Italians, but the important difference in law was now that between rich and poor, *honestiores* and *humiliores.*

Caracalla was succeeded by another African emperor, Macrinus, a Moor who had trained as a lawyer and then joined the army in search of better prospects. He was an innovation in one important respect, being the first non-senator to become emperor. But he did not reign for long. He failed to defeat the Parthian counter-attack in 217 and was forced to seek a humiliating peace. Then, early the following year, the Syrian legions restored the Severan family to power in the person of Caracalla's niece's son Elagabalus.

Elagabalus was only 14 years old at the time, and real power rested with his mother and grandmother, both Syrian princesses, the latter of them the sister of Severus's empress Julia Domna. While they and their officials ran the business of government, Elagabalus devoted himself to his role as hereditary High Priest of the sun god of Emesa. The sacred black stone of Emesa, symbol of the god, was brought to Rome and installed in a special temple on the Palatine. Elagabalus himself engaged in exotic rituals and strange sexual practices in the service of his god. When these became such an embarrassment that they posed a threat to the regime, he was done away with and his more acceptable (though still very young) cousin Severus Alexander made emperor in his place.

It was during the weak reign of Severus Alexander that the first signs emerged of the serious external pressures which were to bring the empire almost to its knees in the decades to come. One of the most important of these events was the establishment of a new imperial power on the eastern frontier. Since the last centuries BC the Near East beyond the limits of Roman rule had been dominated by the empire of the Parthians. In AD 226, the last Parthian king, Artabanus V, was overthrown by one of his vassals, the Persian ruler Ardashir. In the 6th century BC the Persians had conquered the lands around the East Mediterranean, including Asia Minor and Egypt, and Ardashir in a show of bravado now laid claim to these former territories. In 230 he invaded Roman territory, forcing the unwarlike Severus Alexander to stage a powerful counter-attack. It was enough to halt Ardashir in his tracks, but failed to win any great victories. When two years later (235) Alexander preferred do a deal with the Germans on the Rhine frontier rather than fight them, his soldiers decided they had had enough. They murdered Alexander and his mother, and proclaimed as emperor one of their own commanders, Maximinus the Thracian.

The Slide towards Crisis

The army had always been a major power-broker in the imperial game, but the policies of the Severans and their rejection of senatorial authority had made the office of emperor more dependent on the military than ever before. The relationship became even closer during the middle decades of the 3rd century, when the continual threat of foreign invasion made control of the army and military competence the essential prerequisites for a successful reign. The Roman empire was now clearly on the defensive. Those emperors who failed met a speedy and violent end.

The drift towards military autocracy is well represented by Severus Alexander's successor Maximinus. He was neither senator nor equestrian, but an ordinary soldier who had risen through the ranks. Faced with the threat of German invasion, he spent most of his reign on the Rhine and the Danube, and ignored Rome entirely. His place was with the army, not courting politicians in the capital. His only visit to Italy as emperor was at the end of his reign, when the Senate put up two of their own candidates to oppose him. Even on that occasion he didn't reach Rome, but was murdered while besieging the rebellious city of Aquileia (at the head of the Adriatic) in April 238.

The emperors who ruled Rome from Philip the Arab (244–9) to Gallienus (253–68) presided over a situation of increasing crisis. The military struggle was made all the more difficult by the need to defend several frontiers simultaneously. In the west, a German confederation known as the Alemanni threatened the Rhine and Upper Danube. On the lower Danube, the principal enemy was the Goths (another Germanic people, recently settled in the Ukraine). In the east, the Persians under a new aggressive ruler, Shapur I, mounted periodic invasions of Syria and adjacent provinces. The nadir was reached in 260. In that year, the Emperor Valerian was captured by the Persians and ended his days in captivity. No longer able to control the east, his son Gallienus was forced to rely on help from the rulers of Palmyra, who used their position to establish a quasi-independent state. At the same time the western provinces broke away to form a separate Gallic empire, and the truncated body of the central empire was afflicted by a rash of pretenders.

Against all expectations, the empire was slowly put to rights by a series of soldier-emperors of Balkan origin, referred to as the Illyrian emperors. Claudius II (268–70) defeated the Goths. Aurelian (270–75) suppressed the breakaway Palmyrene and Gallic realms and reunited the empire as a single unit. Carus (282–3) turned the tables on the Persians by invading Mesopotamia and sacking the important city of Ctesiphon. But the Roman empire did not escape from its ordeal unscathed. Large areas suffered invasion and destruction, and there was widespread economic dislocation.

Saints and Martyrs

Above: the economic collapse of the mid-3rd century led, in the Western provinces, to a proliferation of imitations of the official Roman coinage. These are often known as "barbarous radiates" on account of their crude style and the radiate crown which is the most prominent feature of the design. They do not appear to have been forgeries in the sense of coins intended to deceive—many are far smaller than their Roman prototypes—and are probably the result of local initiatives to provide small change, suitable for everyday transactions, that the state was unable or unwilling to supply.

Christianity was by no means a new religion in the 3rd century, but began at this time to feature increasingly prominently in the affairs of the empire. The first great Christian persecution was that ordered by the emperor Decius in 250. Christians incurred official displeasure (along with Jews) because they refused to offer traditional pagan sacrifice for the welfare of empire and emperors. But Jewish beliefs were tolerated, whereas Christians were persecuted, ostensibly on the charge of "atheism". We hear of famous public martyrdoms from the 2nd century onwards: of the slave-girl Blandina and her colleagues in the amphitheatre at Lyons in 177; or of Perpetua and Felicity at Carthage in 203, to celebrate the birthday of Severus's son Geta. The persecution of 250, however, was on an altogether different scale, and was followed by a second imperial edict in 257, forbidding public worship, and a third in 258 which was directed against Church leaders and Church property.

Yet despite these persecutions (which were enforced to differing degrees in different provinces) Christianity continued to win new converts, and the deaths of martyrs, although a deterrent, added a touch of heroic lustre.

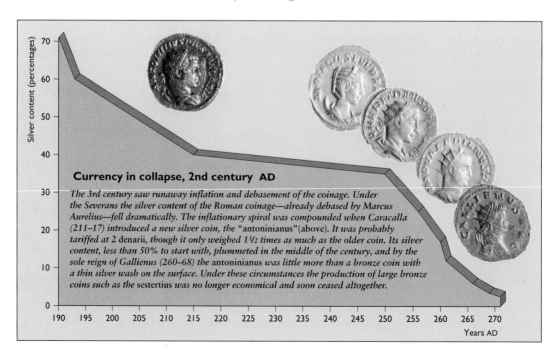

Currency in collapse, 2nd century AD

The 3rd century saw runaway inflation and debasement of the coinage. Under the Severans the silver content of the Roman coinage—already debased by Marcus Aurelius—fell dramatically. The inflationary spiral was compounded when Caracalla (211–17) introduced a new silver coin, the "antoninianus"(above). It was probably tariffed at 2 denarii, though it only weighed 1½ times as much as the older coin. Its silver content, less than 50% to start with, plummeted in the middle of the century, and by the sole reign of Gallienus (260–68) the antoninianus was little more than a bronze coin with a thin silver wash on the surface. Under these circumstances the production of large bronze coins such as the sestertius was no longer economical and soon ceased altogether.

Silver content (percentages): 70, 60, 50, 40, 30, 20, 10, 0

Years AD: 190, 195, 200, 205, 210, 215, 220, 225, 230, 235, 240, 245, 250, 255, 260, 265, 270

Persecution was suspended in 260, an admission of failure on the part of the authorities, and for the next 40 years the Christians were left in peace. Christianity was by now recognized to be more than just another Oriental cult, but it was still very much a minority religion in the empire as a whole. The attempts to stamp it out were harsh and violent, invoking prison, torture and death, but they must be judged in the context of the 3rd century crisis. Christianity could all too easily be seen as yet another force for division in a realm which the emperors were fighting desperately to hold together. Few could have predicted that, within a century, it would have become the official state religion.

Below: *Portchester Castle near Portsmouth is the best-preserved of the chain of coastal forts built on both sides of the English Channel in the late 3rd and early 4th centuries. The rounded projecting towers are typical of later Roman military architecture. In the 4th century this and the other coastal forts were placed under the command of a single military officer, the* comes litoris Saxonici—Count *of the Saxon Shore—whose job was to protect eastern Britain from the activities of Saxon pirates.*

The Year of the Six Emperors

Above: *the eventual victor of the civil wars of 193–7 was Septimius Severus (r.193–211). Born at Lepcis Magna in North Africa, he was prefect of Upper Pannonia when proclaimed emperor by his troops. This portrait appears on a* sestertius *struck later in his reign.*

The assassination of Commodus shattered the political stability of the preceding century and plunged the empire into civil war.

The bloodthirsty eccentricities of the Emperor Commodus (180–92) made him unpopular with aristocracy and court officials alike, and he was eventually murdered on the last day of 192. His successor was the Prefect of Rome, Pertinax, but he too was assassinated just three months later. Power then passed to a rich senator called Didius Julianus in return for a huge bribe to the praetorian guard. The commanders of the frontier armies were unwilling to accept this state of affairs, and in April 193 two rival emperors were proclaimed: Pescennius Niger in the east and Septimius Severus on the Danube. Severus marched quickly on Rome and overthrew Julianus. After only a brief pause to settle affairs in the capital, he then marched east to confront Niger. His army crossed the Sea of Marmara and defeated Niger's forces at Cyzicus and Nicaea. They pressed forward through Asia Minor, overwhelming Niger in a final, decisive encounter at Issus, the same spot where Alexander the Great had defeated the Persians 500 years earlier.

Niger fled to Antioch, where he was captured and killed. Severus spent a few months consolidating his hold on the eastern provinces and mounting a short campaign against the Parthians (▶ *pages 98–9*). Before returning to Rome he went to confront another rival: Clodius Albinus, the governor of Britain. Albinus and Severus had become allies in 193, but by the end of 195 they were openly hostile, and war broke out the following year. Albinus had the army of Britain at his command, but failed to win over the powerful German legions. Severus defeated him outside Lyon in February 197, bringing an end to four years of civil unrest.

The Events of 193

31 Dec 192	Commodus assassinated.
1 Jan 193	Praetorian guard proclaim the City Prefect of Rome, P. Helvius Pertinax, emperor. Their choice is ratified by the Senate.
28 Mar	Pertinax, forced to make unpopular economies, is assassinated by the praetorian guard. Didius Julianus, a rich senator, is proclaimed emperor in return for 25,000 *sesterces* to each praetorian.
Apr–May	G. Pescennius Niger, legate of Syria, and P. Septimius Severus, legate of Pannonia, both proclaimed emperor by their troops. Severus marches on Rome. Senate condemns Julianus and ratifies nomination of Severus.
2 June	Didius Julianus executed
10 June	Septimius Severus enters Rome at the head of his troops.

Above and right:
Severus's predecessors and rivals, as depicted on their silver coins. From top: Publius Helvius Pertinax; Marcus Didius Julianus and Gaius Pescennius Niger.

Britan

Albinus crosses
to Gaul with a

Lugdunen
Liger
Loire

A

19 Feb 197
Severan forces defe
Albinus in bat
outside Ly
Albinus commits suicid
Tarr
Tarrag

Lusitania

Emerita Augusta o
Merida

Tarraconensis
Corduba
o Cordoba

Baetica

Gades o
Cadiz

o Tingi
Tangier

Carthago N
Cartagena

Caesarea

Mauretania

N

| 0 | 450 kms |
| 0 | 300 miles |

Clodius Albinus (below) was Severus's longest-lived rival. Severus granted him the title Caesar in 193, but when Albinus was proclaimed Augustus by his troops in 195, war between the two emperors was inevitable. Albinus set up his government at Lyon, capital of Gallia Lugduniensis and one of the great cities of the Roman west (right, the theatre). After his defeat by Severus just outside the city early in 197, Albinus committed suicide.

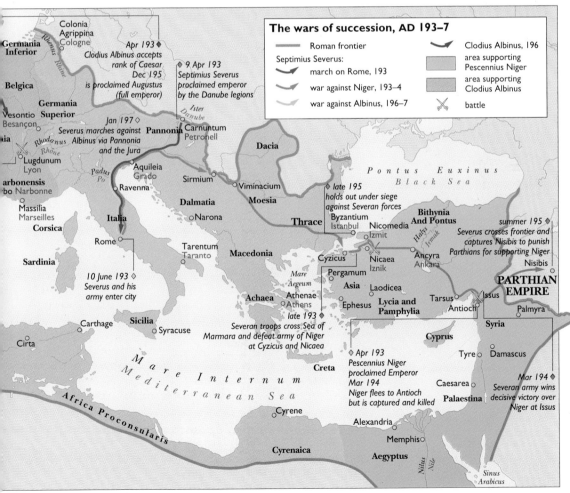

The wars of succession, AD 193–7

— Roman frontier

Septimius Severus:
↘ march on Rome, 193
↘ war against Niger, 193–4
↘ war against Albinus, 196–7

↘ Clodius Albinus, 196

area supporting Pescennius Niger

area supporting Clodius Albinus

✗ battle

Apr 193 ◆
Clodius Albinus accepts rank of Caesar
Dec 195
is proclaimed Augustus (full emperor)

◆ **9 Apr 193**
Septimius Severus proclaimed emperor by the Danube legions

Jan 197 ◆
Severus marches against Albinus via Pannonia and the Jura

◆ **late 195**
holds out under siege against Severan forces

summer 195 ◆
Severus crosses frontier and captures Nisibis to punish Parthians for supporting Niger

10 June 193 ◆
Severus and his army enter city

late 193 ◆
Severan troops cross Sea of Marmara and defeat army of Niger at Cyzicus and Nicaea

◆ **Apr 193**
Pescennius Niger proclaimed Emperor
Mar 194
Niger flees to Antioch but is captured and killed

Mar 194 ◆
Severan army wins decisive victory over Niger at Issus

Colonia Agrippina Cologne
Germania Inferior
Rhenus Rhine
Belgica
Germania Superior
Vesontio Besançon
Rhodanus Rhône
...ia
Lugdunum Lyon
...arbonensis
...bo Narbonne
Massilia Marseilles
Corsica
Padus Po
Aquileia Grado
Ravenna
Italia
Rome
Sardinia
Carthage
Cirta
Sicilia
Syracuse
Tarentum Taranto
Ister Danube
Pannonia
Carnuntum Petronell
Sirmium
Viminacium
Dalmatia
Narona
Macedonia
Achaea
Athenae Athens
Dacia
Moesia
Thrace
Byzantium Istanbul
Nicomedia Izmit
Nicaea Iznik
Cyzicus
Pergamum
Asia
Ephesus
Pontus Euxinus Black Sea
Bithynia And Pontus
Ancyra Ankara
Halys Kizil Irmak
Laodicea
Lycia and Pamphylia
Tarsus
Antioch
Issus
Cyprus
Tyre
Caesarea
Palaestina
PARTHIAN EMPIRE
Nisibis
Palmyra
Syria
Damascus
Mare Aegeum
Creta
Cyrene
Mare Internum Mediterranean Sea
Africa Proconsularis
Cyrenaica
Alexandria
Memphis
Aegyptus
Nilus Nile
Sinus Arabicus

The Parthian Wars

Above: a contemporary portrait bust of the Emperor Caracalla (r. 211–17). On the death of Septimius Severus, Caracalla inherited the throne jointly with his brother Geta, but promptly murdered him. Caracalla's reputation for cruelty was increased by his unexplained massacre of the young men of Alexandria in the spring of 216.

Civil strife among Rome's eastern rivals, the Parthians, allowed the emperors Severus and Caracalla to expand their territory.

Rome's eastern frontier ran up against the empire of the Parthians, who had progressively taken control of Iran and Mesopotamia in the final centuries BC. They had inflicted a crushing defeat on the Roman general Crassus at Carrhae in 53 BC, and had inflicted heavy casualties on Mark Antony's retreating army in 36 BC. By the 2nd century AD, however, they were no longer the force they had been. Trajan successfully invaded Mesopotamia in 114, and briefly controlled the whole country. Half a century later, during the joint reign of Marcus Aurelius and Lucius Verus, the Romans invaded again and sacked Ctesiphon, the Parthian capital of Mesopotamia.

During the reign of Septimius Severus (193–211) the Parthian realm was riven by internal political divisions and proved even easier prey. Severus conducted a short campaign in northern Mesopotamia in 195 to punish the Parthians for supporting his rival Pescennius Niger (▶ pages 96–97). Nisibis was captured, and a new Roman province of Osrhoene established. Two years later he was back again, sacking Ctesiphon for the second time in 50 years and taking a further chunk of Parthian territory to form the Roman province of Mesopotamia.

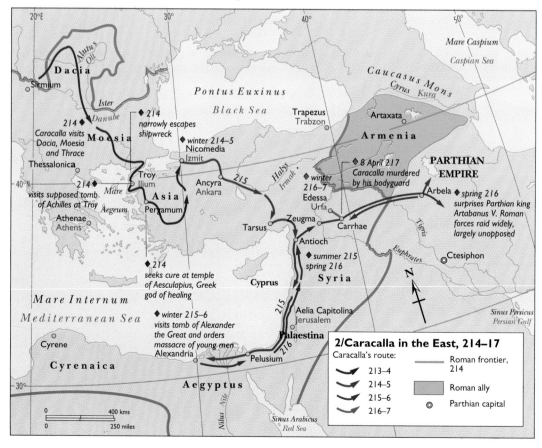

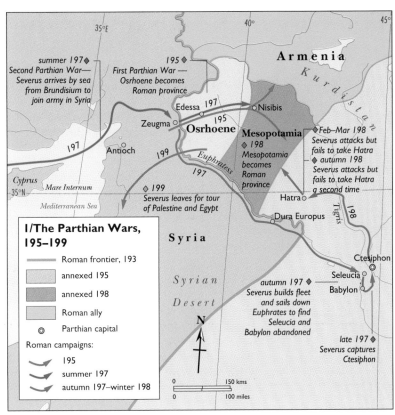

"[Severus] constructed boats on the Euphrates and proceeded forward partly by sailing and partly by marching along the river... Later, upon capturing Ctesiphon, he permitted the soldiers to plunder the entire city, and he slew a vast number of people, besides taking as many as a hundred thousand captives."
Cassius Dio,
Roman History

I/The Parthian Wars, 195–199

- Roman frontier, 193
- annexed 195
- annexed 198
- Roman ally
- ◎ Parthian capital

Roman campaigns:
- 195
- summer 197
- autumn 197–winter 198

summer 197 ◆ Second Parthian War— Severus arrives by sea from Brundisium to join army in Syria

195 ◆ First Parthian War — Osrhoene becomes Roman province

Feb–Mar 198 ◆ Severus attacks but fails to take Hatra
autumn 198 ◆ Severus attacks but fails to take Hatra a second time

◆ 198 Mesopotamia becomes Roman province

◆ 199 Severus leaves for tour of Palestine and Egypt

autumn 197 ◆ Severus builds fleet and sails down Euphrates to find Seleucia and Babylon abandoned

late 197 ◆ Severus captures Ctesiphon

Edessa · Zeugma · Antioch · Nisibis · Osrhoene · Mesopotamia · Armenia · Kurdistan · Cyprus · Mare Internum · Mediterranean Sea · Syria · Syrian Desert · Euphrates · Hatra · Dura Europus · Tigris · Ctesiphon · Seleucia · Babylon

0   150 kms
0   100 miles

Below: *Dura Europus, on the west bank of the Euphrates, was captured by the Romans in 165 and became a strategic frontier town. The citadel served as both an inner refuge and as a strongpoint controlling the river traffic.*

The next major development came under Severus's son and successor Caracalla (211–17). Caracalla spent much of his reign travelling through the eastern provinces. His main objective was a further invasion of Parthia, which he began in 216 with a surprise attack on Arbela in Media, beyond the River Tigris. Although the Parthians were yet again weakened by rival claimants to the throne, they struck back in 217 and forced the Romans to come to terms. By that time, however, Caracalla was dead, murdered on the road from Edessa to Carrhae.

The City of Rome under the Severans

As capital of a great empire, the city of Rome was the site of massive building projects in the first three centuries AD.

Among the most spectacular were a series of bathing establishments, beginning with those of Trajan but best represented today by the remains of the Baths of Caracalla. Entertainment of a different kind was provided by the Colosseum, the largest amphitheatre of the Roman world, capable of seating some 50,000 spectators (▶ *pages 82–3*). Nearby, in the heart of the city, were the Imperial Fora, a series of temples and administrative buildings built by successive emperors to complement and expand the facilities of the original Forum Romanum. The emperors also also built for their own comfort, and Septimius Severus (AD 193–211) added his own palace to those of his predecessors on the Palatine Hill. Imperial monuments of a different kind were the temples to the deified emperors and the great circular imperial mausolea built by Augustus and Hadrian.

Above: this fragment of a marble map of Rome shows part of the Aventine Hill, with the temples of Diana Cornificiana and Minerva. The map was made around AD 200 and shows the rebuilding of the area round the Forum Pacis, which had been damaged by fire some some years earlier. It was originally displayed there in a hall near the Temple of Peace.

Throughout this period Rome was unwalled, confident and secure at the heart of a powerful empire. It was therefore a sign of more troubled times when in 271 the Emperor Aurelian ordered the construction of the great circuit of defensive walls and gates which bears his name. In the following 50 years Rome received new buildings from Diocletian and Constantine, but by the middle of the 4th century the centres of power had moved elsewhere and the city was in decline.

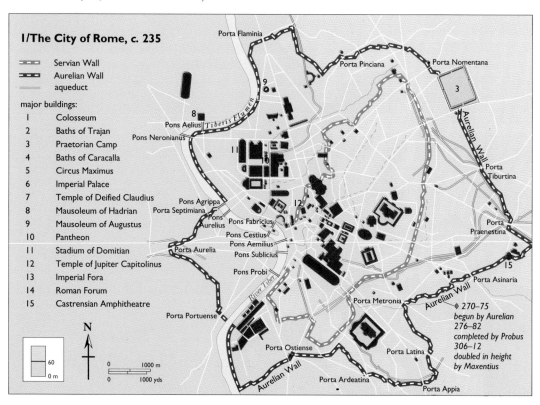

I/The City of Rome, c. 235

- ▭▭▭ Servian Wall
- ▭▭▭ Aurelian Wall
- ―――― aqueduct

major buildings:

1. Colosseum
2. Baths of Trajan
3. Praetorian Camp
4. Baths of Caracalla
5. Circus Maximus
6. Imperial Palace
7. Temple of Deified Claudius
8. Mausoleum of Hadrian
9. Mausoleum of Augustus
10. Pantheon
11. Stadium of Domitian
12. Temple of Jupiter Capitolinus
13. Imperial Fora
14. Roman Forum
15. Castrensian Amphitheatre

N

60
0 m

0   1000 m
0   1000 yds

Porta Flaminia
Porta Pinciana
Porta Nomentana
Porta Tiburtina
Porta Praenestina
Porta Asinaria
Aurelian Wall
Pons Aelius
Tiberis Flumen
Pons Neronianus
Pons Agrippa
Porta Septimiana
Pons Aurelius
Pons Fabricius
Pons Cestius
Pons Aemilius
Pons Sublicius
Porta Aurelia
Pons Probi
River Tiber
Porta Portuense
Porta Metronia
Aurelian Wall
Porta Ostiense
Porta Latina
Porta Ardeatina
Porta Appia
Aurelian Wall

◆ 270–75
begun by Aurelian
276–82
completed by Probus
306–12
doubled in height
by Maxentius

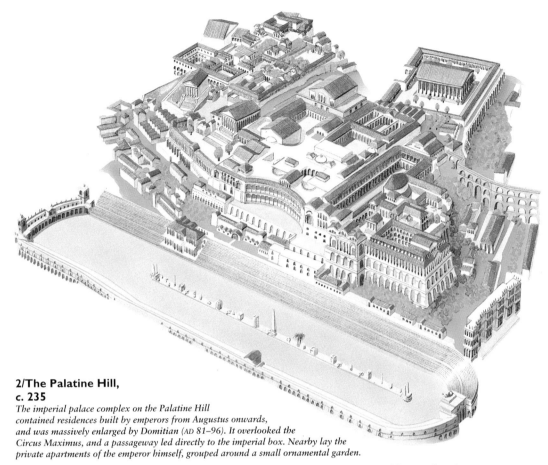

2/The Palatine Hill, c. 235

*The imperial palace complex on the Palatine Hill
contained residences built by emperors from Augustus onwards,
and was massively enlarged by Domitian (AD 81–96). It overlooked the
Circus Maximus, and a passageway led directly to the imperial box. Nearby lay the
private apartments of the emperor himself, grouped around a small ornamental garden.*

*Guarded by the praetorian guard (who had their own walled camp on the northeastern edge of the city), the Palatine
remained the principal residence of the emperors into the 3rd century. By this time, the hilltop was crowded with
buildings; to make room for his own residence, Septimius Severus had to build a massive vaulted platform out from
the side of the hill. This was partly concealed by a free-standing ornamental façade, the Septizonium, at ground
level. On the northwest side of the hill, a later Severan emperor Elagabalus (218–22) added a vast temple.*

*Right: in the south of the city,
the Emperor Caracalla
(211–17) built the largest and
most extravagant baths Rome
had yet seen. These were the
leisure complexes of their age,
complete with art galleries,
libraries and exercise halls.
Lavishly decorated with
marble and mosaics, the Baths
of Caracalla could hold up to
1500 people.*

Mystery Cults

The traditional Roman gods were gradually overshadowed by Oriental "mystery" cults and their deities: Cybele, Isis, Mithras—and Christ.

"And now comes in a procession/ Devotees of the frenzied Bellona, and Cybele, Mother of Gods/Led by a giant eunuch, the idol of his lesser/ Companions in obscenity. Long ago, with a sherd,/ He sliced off his genitals: now neither the howling rabble/Nor the kettledrums can outshriek him."

Juvenal,
Satire VI

The religious beliefs of ancient Rome were mixed and varied. At their heart lay the traditional pantheon of Roman gods, headed by Jupiter and Juno. During the later Republic, these came increasingly to be equated with Greek deities of similar function, Juno, for example, being considered the Roman equivalent of Hera, and Diana of Artemis. The Romans also adopted a number of Greek gods, including Apollo.

The most significant newcomers in Roman religious life during the late Republic were not however Greek gods or rituals, but cults of a more distant, Oriental origin. These reflected the growth of Roman political influence in the east Mediterranean; but the earliest of these introductions, the cult of Cybele or Magna Mater, took place when the Romans had hardly set foot east of the Adriatic. This was in 204, during the second Punic War, when the black stone of Cybele was brought from her sanctuary at Pessinus in Anatolia and installed in a temple on the Palatine, in obedience to a prophecy which foretold she would help the Romans against Hannibal.

Other Oriental cults followed the introduction of Cybele to Rome. One was that of Atargatis, a fertility deity often referred to simply as the "Syrian goddess". There were also Egyptian deities, notably Isis and Serapis, the latter developed from the cult of the sacred Apis bulls at Memphis. These were brought to Rome through commercial contacts and though generally discouraged by the state, they spread throughout the empire in the early centuries AD.

These cults drew their popularity from the fact that they offered their adherents the hope of immortality and a more personal and spiritual belief than the official state religion. Each cult had its own special features. The worship of Cybele, for example, was famous for the ritual of *taurobolium*, in which the individual stepped down into a pit where he or she was bathed in the blood of a bull sacrificed above them. This was clearly a ceremony of purification, though sometimes performed on behalf of the emperor and the state.

Right: the god Mithras was of Persian origin, and became particularly popular with the Roman army. He was depicted in his shrines slaying the mystic bull whose blood was the source of life. Mithraic believers sought moral purification through undergoing physical ordeals.

Right: *many popular cults originated in the eastern provinces. This fresco, from the Temple of Conon at Dura Europus in Syria, dedicated in* AD 70, *shows priests, wearing conical hats, lighting a sacrificial fire.*

Below right: *during the centuries of suppression, Christians used secret symbols. Scratched on this tile from Corinium (Cirencester in Gloucestershire) is an apparently innocent word game: "Arepo the sower guides the wheels carefully" readable either vertically or horizontally. But the Latin words are an anagram of* Pater Noster, A O *(alpha and omega). The Cirencester tile cannot be dated accurately, but a fragment of the same palindrome has been found on a late 2nd-century amphora sherd from the Roman fort at Manchester.*

Below: *the cult of the Syrian sun god was introduced to Rome in 218 by the Emperor Elagabalus. Reintroduced by Aurelian later in the century, it became an important part in the state religion. This lead plaque shows the sun god in his chariot; a female divinity flanked by horsemen below and, at the base, a banquet scene. Found in the former Yugoslavia, it dates from the late 3rd or early 4th century when the cult was at its height.*

"Mysteries", sacred truths revealed only to the initiated, were a feature of many cults, and made conversion an emotive experience. This is true of two other eastern religions which became widespread in the early empire: Mithraism and Christianity. During the 3rd century the state religion itself became merged with eastern beliefs. Aurelian (270–5) built a huge temple at Rome to Sol Invictus (the Unconquered Sun). This cult remained a key element of official worship until the conversion of the Emperor Constantine in the early 4th century, marked the final stage in the victory of Oriental religion over the traditional Roman gods (▶ *page 124–5*).

Right: *this relief from Rome carving from Rome shows an* archigallus, *the eunuch high priest of the cult of Cybele, also known as Magna Mater. Wearing the robes and mitre of his calling, he carries a flail—the rites involved flagellation—and a vessel of pine kernels, which were sacred to the goddess. Around him are the musical instruments used to drive the worshippers into a frenzy of ecstatic dancing.*

Roman Africa

The North African provinces, from the borders of Egypt to the Atlantic coast, were among the most prosperous in the empire.

"Throughout its inhabited area it is extraordinarily fertile, but, since the greater part of it is uncultivated and covered by sterile sands ... it is more abandoned than settled."
Pomponius Mela on Africa

With the Sahara Desert to the south and the Mediterranean to the north, the African provinces were fertile lands with sufficient rainfall for farming, backed up by irrigation where necessary. Olives and cereals were the principal crops, and both were widely exported. Roman North Africa was second only to Egypt as a supplier of grain for Rome, and such was the abundance of olive oil that only the poorest households were unable to afford oil lamps to light their homes. The great cities lay mostly in the old Carthaginian lands of the east. Thysdrus (El Djem) and Lepcis Magna were prosperous oil producers, but the greatest of all African cities was Carthage.

North Africa possessed one notable advantage over the European or Levantine provinces of the empire, in that its long land frontier was less threatened by foreign enemies and demanded considerably fewer troops. A system of forts and military roads was built, nonetheless, to form a protective shield against nomadic raiders, and physical barriers were erected at specially vulnerable places or across seasonal pastoral routes leading south into the desert. There were occasional raids, even so, but the relative security of North Africa is shown by the fact that only a single legion was stationed there, compared with 14 or more on the Rhine–Danube frontier.

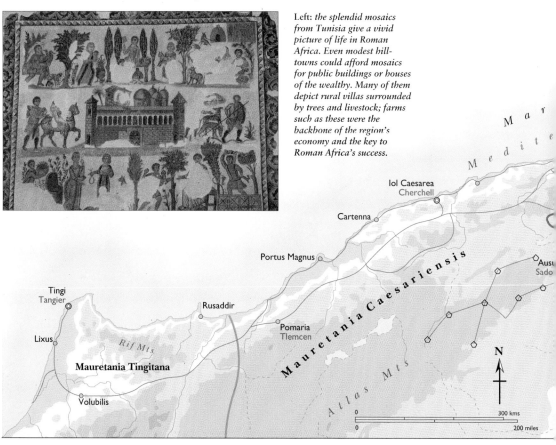

Left: *the splendid mosaics from Tunisia give a vivid picture of life in Roman Africa. Even modest hill-towns could afford mosaics for public buildings or houses of the wealthy. Many of them depict rural villas surrounded by trees and livestock; farms such as these were the backbone of the region's economy and the key to Roman Africa's success.*

2/Olive oil extraction

The olive oil on which much of Roman Africa's wealth was based was extracted at countless farms throughout the provinces. This oil processing building was excavated at Wadi umm el-Bagel in modern Libya. The "arbores" in Room 1 held a wooden beam with a weight at the other end. This was used to press the olives. The oil would run into a tank full of water, where the sediment sank to the bottom. The oil floated on the top and drained through a gully into a tank. The best oil would be ladelled into vats, while the heavier grade oil went through a spout to Room 5, where amphorae (storage jars) were waiting to receive it.

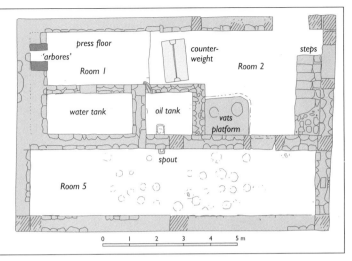

press floor
'arbores'
Room 1
counter-weight
Room 2
steps
water tank
oil tank
vats platform
Room 5
spout

0 1 2 3 4 5 m

1/Roman Africa, 3rd century AD

- ▦▦▦ province
- ◉ provincial capital
- ◈ legionary base
- ○ other centre
- —— Roman road
- ◇ frontier fort
- ▬▬ frontier barrier

Right: by the 3rd century AD, Thysdrus (El Djem) in modern Tunisia had grown so wealthy on the profits of olive oil that it was able to build an amphitheatre surpassed in size only by the Colosseum at Rome.

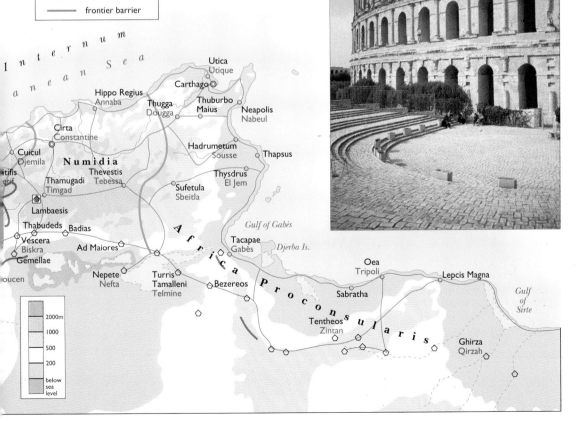

Internum Mare
Mediterranean Sea

Utica
Utique
Carthago
Hippo Regius
Annaba
Thugga
Dougga
Thuburbo Maius
Neapolis
Nabeul
Cirta
Constantine
Cuicul
Djemila
Numidia
Thevestis
Tebessa
Hadrumetum
Sousse
Thapsus
Thamugadi
Timgad
Sufetula
Sbeitla
Thysdrus
El Jem
Lambaesis
Thabudeds
Badias
Véscera
Biskra
Gemellae
Ad Maiores
Africa
Gulf of Gabès
Tacapae
Gabès
Djerba Is.
Nepete
Nefta
Turris Tamalleni
Telmine
Bezereos
Proconsularis
Oea
Tripoli
Lepcis Magna
Sabratha
Gulf of Sirte
Tentheos
Zintan
Ghirza
Qirzah

2000m
1000
500
200
below sea level

Three African Cities

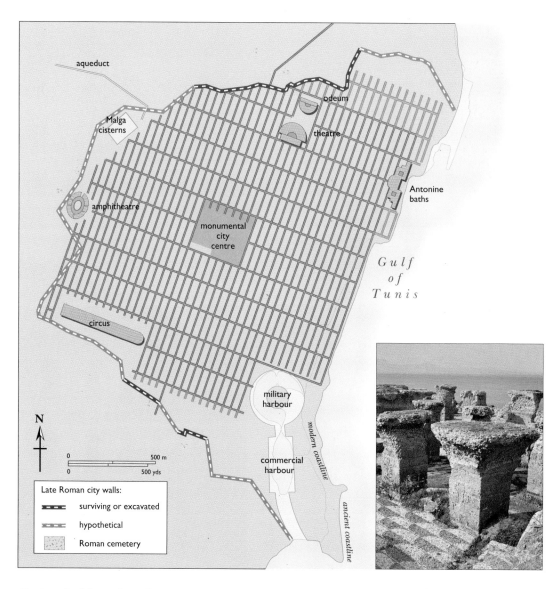

Late Roman city walls:

- ▪▪▪ surviving or excavated
- ▪▪▪ hypothetical
- ▒▒ Roman cemetery

Carthage had been Rome's great enemy during the three Punic Wars, and was destroyed by them in 146 BC. It was too good a site to be ignored, however, and in 29 BC the Emperor Augustus officially founded a new Roman city of Carthage. It soon grew to be one of the four greatest cities of the Roman world, alongside Alexandria, Antioch and Rome itself. The Emperor Hadrian augmented the city's water supply by constructing the impressive Zaghouan aqueduct in the mid-2nd century, and his successor Antoninus Pius donated the immense Antonine baths overlooking the sea front. Carthage became a wealthy and sophisticated metropolis, and by the 3rd century had gained additional standing as a centre of Christianity. The city was captured by the Vandals in 439, but remained a major centre until the 7th century, when it was eclipsed by the new Arab foundation of Tunis nearby.

Above: the hypocaust piers of the Antonine baths on the waterfront at Carthage. Built on the instructions of the Emperor Antoninus Pius between AD 145 and 162, this magnificent baths complex was one of the largest outside Rome itself.

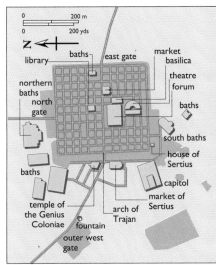

Timgad is one of the finest examples of a Roman *colonia*, a city created specially for retired soldiers of the Third Augustan Legion who were based at Lambaesis nearby. The city was founded in AD 100 by order of the Emperor Trajan; its rigid geometrical plan testifies to its military origin. Within the grid, space was found for a forum, theatre and public baths, but other buildings such as the Capitolium (a temple to the Capitoline triad of Jupiter, Juno and Minerva) were relegated to the suburbs. Colonies such as Timgad were intended to serve as strongpoints for the surrounding area, and the city was provided with walls from the start. As it grew, Timgad acquired all the usual amenities of a prosperous Roman city, including a library and no fewer than 14 public baths. Many houses were decorated with ornate floral mosaics.

Lepcis Magna, like Carthage, was founded as a Phoenician colony and only came under Roman rule in the 2nd century BC. Its wealth derived from a fertile hinterland where cereals and olives were grown, and from the trade which passed through its harbour. By the early 1st century AD the city had been furnished with a new forum and basilica, and a fine theatre and market with twin central kiosks. In the early 2nd century, Trajan and Hadrian added a triumphal arch and public baths respectively. The city reached its greatest distinction at the end of the century when Septimius Severus, born at Lepcis, became Roman emperor. He built a grand new forum and colonnaded street, and improved the harbour facilities by adding warehouses and a lighthouse.

Above: *the theatre at Lepcis Magna was built in AD 1–2 by a Punic nobleman Annobal Rufus and refurbished in the 2nd century.*

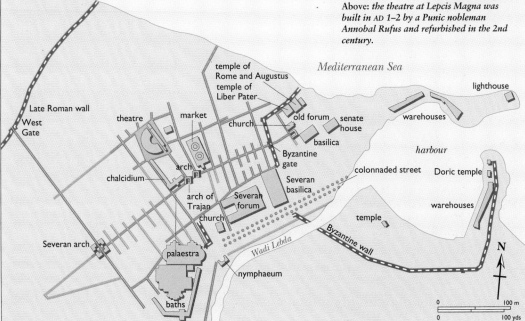

The Empire at Bay

The middle of the 3rd century saw the Roman Empire threatened by internal strife and foreign invasions.

"Three hundred and twenty thousand Goths have invaded Roman territory... The whole republic is fatigued and exhausted."
Life of Claudius II, from the Historia Augusta

In the eastern provinces the main adversaries were the Goths and the Persians. The Goths were a Germanic people who had recently settled around the northern shores of the Black Sea. From the 240s to the 270s they posed a continuous menace to the Balkan provinces and Asia Minor. They defeated and killed the Emperor Decius in 251 at Abrittus, but did not attempt to settle within the imperial frontier. In 256 they mounted maritime raids on Asia Minor, and in 268 launched a combined land and sea offensive, sacking Athens. The Persians had overthrown their Parthian overlords in the 220s to establish a new empire east of the Euphrates. They staged a series of assaults on Rome's eastern provinces from the 230s, culminating in the great invasions of 253, when Antioch was sacked, and 260, when they took the Emperor Valerian prisoner at Edessa. In addition to foreign attack Valerian's son Gallienus (r. 253–68) was also challenged by a succession of rivals. Some aimed at total power, while others formed breakaway states in the east and west.

Germanic peoples broke through the western frontiers on several occasions, most seriously in 260 when they invaded Gaul and raiding parties reached as far as Tarraco in Spain. There were major invasions of Italy in 259, 268 and 271. The Romans fought back successfully on all fronts, however; within a few years the Persians had been driven back beyond the Tigris and the Goths beyond the Danube. By the end of the 270s the empire had been reunited and its frontiers restored.

Below: the Emperor Trajan Decius (r. 249–51), depicted on one of the last silver tetradrachms issued by the mint at Antioch, capital of Roman Syria. Two years after Decius's death in battle against the Goths, Antioch was sacked by the Persians and this long-running coin series came to an end.

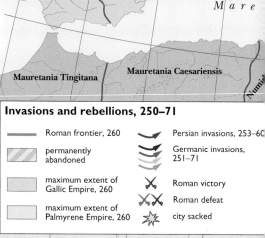

Invasions and rebellions, 250–71

Roman frontier, 260	Persian invasions, 253–60
permanently abandoned	Germanic invasions, 251–71
maximum extent of Gallic Empire, 260	Roman victory
	Roman defeat
maximum extent of Palmyrene Empire, 260	city sacked

Right: the capture of the Emperor Valerian by the Persians in 260 is commemorated in this rock carving at Naqsh-i Rustam, near Persepolis. Valerian died in captivity, and it was rumoured that his stuffed body was displayed as a trophy in the Persian court. True or not, the story reflects the humiliation inflicted on Rome by the capture of the emperor.

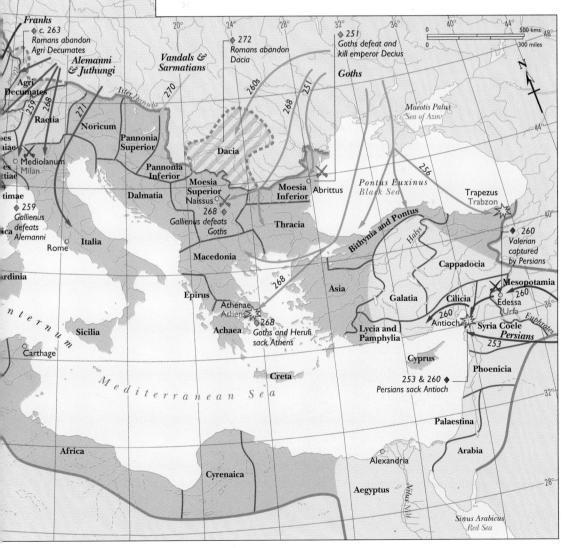

Franks
◆ c. 263
Romans abandon
Agri Decumates

**Alemanni
& Juthungi**

**Vandals &
Sarmatians**

◆ 272
Romans abandon
Dacia

◆ 251
Goths defeat and
kill emperor Decius

Goths

Agri
Decumates

259 268

271

270

260s

268

251

268

256

Maeotis Palus
Sea of Azov

500 kms
300 miles

N

Raetia

Noricum

**Pannonia
Superior**

Ister Danube

**Pannonia
Inferior**

Dacia

○ Mediolanum
Milan

◆ 259
Gallienus
defeats
Alemanni

Dalmatia

**Moesia
Superior**
Naissus ○

**Moesia
Inferior** Abrittus

Trapezus
Trabzon

○ 268
Gallienus defeats
Goths

Thracia

*Pontus Euxinus
Black Sea*

Bithynia and Pontus

Halys

◆ 260
Valerian
captured
by Persians

Rome ○ **Italia**

Macedonia

Cappadocia

dinia

Epirus

268

Asia

Galatia

Cilicia

Mesopotamia
260
Edessa
Urfa

Euphrates

Athenae
Athens

◆ 268
Goths and Heruli
sack Athens

Achaea

Sicilia

**Lycia and
Pamphylia**

260
Antioch

260
Syria Coele
Persians

253

○ Carthage

M e d i t e r r a n e a n   S e a

Creta

Cyprus

253 & 260 ◆
Persians sack Antioch

Phoenicia

Palaestina

Africa

Cyrenaica

Alexandria

Arabia

Aegyptus

Nilus Nile

*Sinus Arabicus
Red Sea*

The West Breaks Away

Alarmed by Rome's failure to defend them from attack, the western provinces break away and choose their own emperor.

Beset by invaders on his northern and eastern frontiers, the Emperor Gallienus (r. 253–68) was unable to hold the empire together. Many provincials preferred to put their faith in regional leaders, who could be seen to be defending their frontiers, than in a distant and ineffectual central authority. The most successful regional ruler was Postumus, governor of Lower Germany, whose revolt in the autumn of 260 led to the creation of a Gallic Empire which survived as a separate state for almost 15 years. The core of this breakaway empire was formed by the three provinces of Gaul (Lugdunensis, Aquitania and Narbonensis) plus the two Germanies with their powerful frontier forces. By 261, Britain and Spain had also gone over to Postumus, and even Raetia was briefly in his control.

The Gallic Empire won support from the people of these provinces by concentrating on the defence of the Rhine frontier; neither Postumus nor any of his successors made an attempt to march on Rome. Instead, they recognized the distinctive personality of the western Roman provinces and sought to make this a source of strength. Prosperous and self-sufficient, the Gallic Empire survived the death of its founder, though Spain seceded in 269 and the lands east of the Rhone were conquered by Claudius II (r. 268–270). Four years later the last Gallic Emperor, Tetricus, was defeated in a hard-fought battle at Châlons-sur-Marne and the provinces of Gaul, Britain and Germany were reabsorbed into the Roman Empire by Claudius's successor Aurelian (r. 270–75).

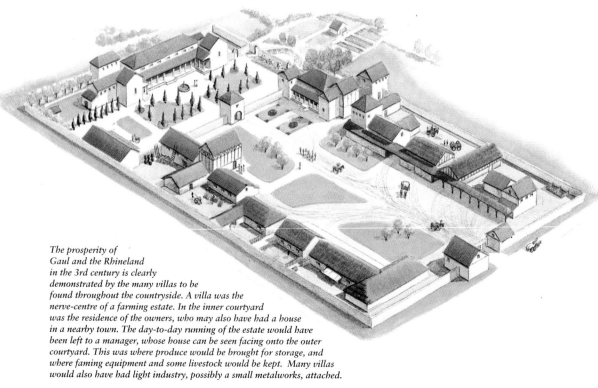

The prosperity of Gaul and the Rhineland in the 3rd century is clearly demonstrated by the many villas to be found throughout the countryside. A villa was the nerve-centre of a farming estate. In the inner courtyard was the residence of the owners, who may also have had a house in a nearby town. The day-to-day running of the estate would have been left to a manager, whose house can be seen facing onto the outer courtyard. This was where produce would be brought for storage, and where faming equipment and some livestock would be kept. Many villas would also have had light industry, possibly a small metalworks, attached.

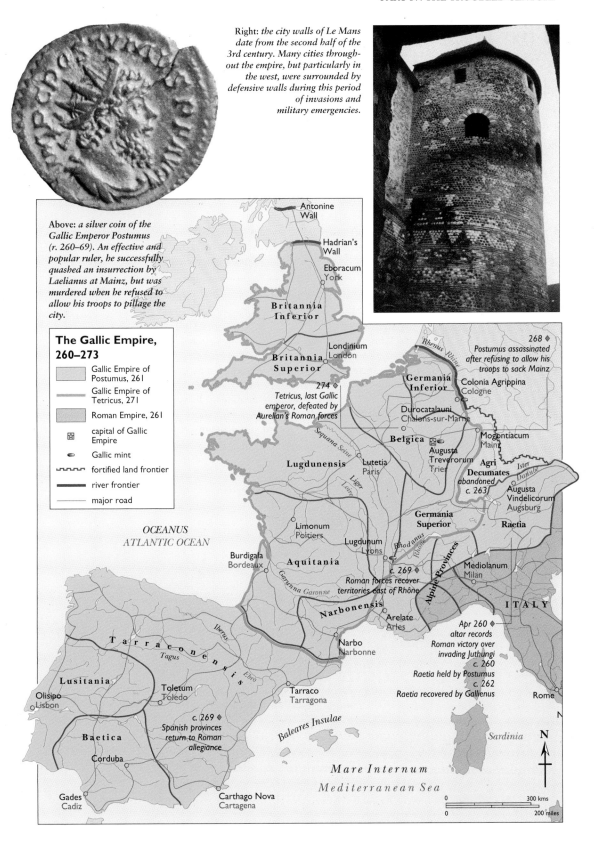

Right: the city walls of Le Mans date from the second half of the 3rd century. Many cities throughout the empire, but particularly in the west, were surrounded by defensive walls during this period of invasions and military emergencies.

Above: a silver coin of the Gallic Emperor Postumus (r. 260–69). An effective and popular ruler, he successfully quashed an insurrection by Laelianus at Mainz, but was murdered when he refused to allow his troops to pillage the city.

The Gallic Empire, 260–273

Gallic Empire of Postumus, 261
Gallic Empire of Tetricus, 271
Roman Empire, 261
capital of Gallic Empire
Gallic mint
fortified land frontier
river frontier
major road

Antonine Wall
Hadrian's Wall
Eboracum York
Britannia Inferior
Britannia Superior
Londinium London

268 ◆ Postumus assassinated after refusing to allow his troops to sack Mainz

Germania Inferior
Colonia Agrippina Cologne

274 ◆ Tetricus, last Gallic emperor, defeated by Aurelian's Roman forces

Durocatalauni Chalons-sur-Marne
Mogontiacum Mainz
Belgica
Augusta Treverorum Trier
Agri Decumates abandoned c. 263
Augusta Vindelicorum Augsburg

Lugdunensis
Lutetia Paris
Sequana Seine
Liger Loire

Germania Superior
Raetia

OCEANUS ATLANTIC OCEAN

Limonum Poitiers
Lugdunum Lyons
Rhodanus Rhône
Mediolanum Milan

Burdigala Bordeaux
Aquitania
c. 269 ◆ Roman forces recover territories east of Rhône
Garunna Garonne

ITALY

Narbonensis
Arelate Arles
Alpine Provinces

Tarraconensis
Tagus
Iberus
Ebro

Apr 260 ◆ altar records Roman victory over invading Juthungi
c. 260 Raetia held by Postumus
c. 262 Raetia recovered by Gallienus

Narbo Narbonne

Lusitania
Olisipo Lisbon
Toletum Toledo

Tarraco Tarragona

Rome

c. 269 ◆ Spanish provinces return to Roman allegiance

Baleares Insulae

Sardinia

Baetica
Corduba

Mare Internum Mediterranean Sea

Gades Cadiz
Carthago Nova Cartagena

0 300 kms
0 200 miles

N

111

The Rise and Fall of Palmyra

As Rome lost its grip on its eastern provinces, the powerful trading city of Palmyra assumed the leadership of the region.

"In the manner of the Persians [Zenobia] received worship... but in the manner of a Roman emperor she came forth to public assemblies, wearing a helmet and girt with a purple fillet ... Her face was dark... her eyes were black and powerful ... her spirit divinely great, her beauty incredible."

The Thirty Tyrants, from the *Historia Augusta*

During the first two and a half centuries AD, the city of Palmyra operated as a semi-independent power on the fringes of Roman Syria, but its great opportunity came when the Persians overran the eastern provinces in 260 and captured the Roman Emperor Valerian at Edessa (▶ *pages 108–9*). Valerian's son Gallienus was distracted by troubles on the northern frontier, by the need to deal with a series of rival claimants, and by the secession of the Gallic Empire, and was unable to counter the Persian threat in person. This left the field clear for the Palmyrenes under their ruler Odenathus to take the lead in defending the eastern provinces. At first they operated as allies of Gallienus, and achieved some notable successes: they recovered the province of Mesopotamia from the Persians, and in 266 defeated them in front of their capital Ctesiphon.

The greatest expansion of Palmyrene power came after Odenathus's death in 267. Although he was nominally succeeded by his son Vaballathus, the real power was exercised by his widow Zenobia. In 270–71 she embarked on a programme of conquest which brought Egypt and large areas of Asia Minor under her rule. It was a short-lived triumph, however, since in 272 the Emperor Aurelian (*r.* 270–75) launched a determined campaign to recover the eastern provinces and destroy Zenobia's power. He advanced through Asia Minor, winning victories at Tyana, Immae, and Emesa, and besieging Zenobia in Palmyra itself. She was caught fleeing to Persia on a camel, and after appearing in Aurelian's triumph was allowed to retire to a villa near Rome. The eastern provinces were brought back peacefully under Roman control, but the Palmyrenes had not learned their lesson. In 273 they tried to assert their independence once again; the revolt was put down and the city destroyed.

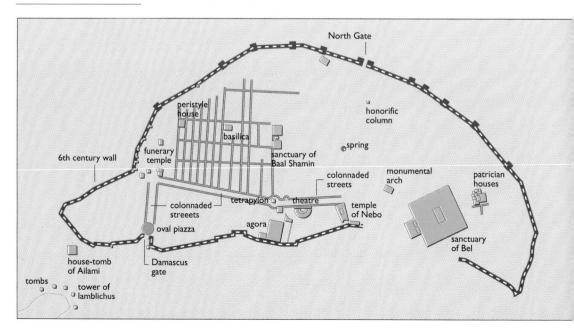

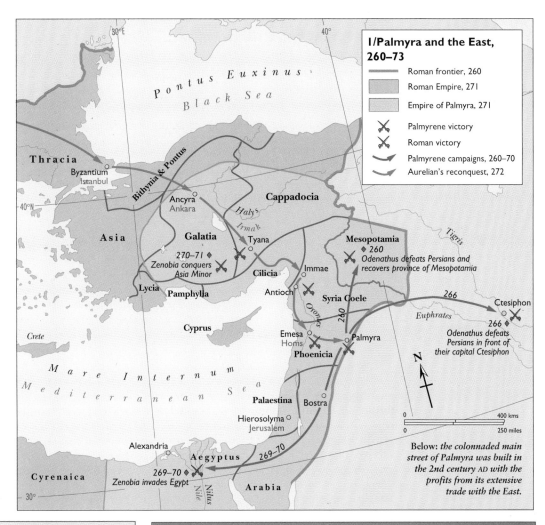

1/Palmyra and the East, 260–73

- Roman frontier, 260
- Roman Empire, 271
- Empire of Palmyra, 271
- ✗ Palmyrene victory
- ✗ Roman victory
- Palmyrene campaigns, 260–70
- Aurelian's reconquest, 272

Pontus Euxinus
Black Sea

Thracia
Byzantium
Istanbul

Bithynia & Pontus

Ancyra
Ankara

Cappadocia

Asia

Galatia

Halys
Irmak

Tyana

270–71 ◆
Zenobia conquers
Asia Minor

Cilicia

Immae

Mesopotamia
◆ 260
Odenathus defeats Persians and
recovers province of Mesopotamia

Tigris

Lycia
Pamphylia

Antioch

Syria Coele

Orontes

260

266

Ctesiphon

Cyprus

Euphrates

266 ◆
Odenathus defeats
Persians in front of
their capital Ctesiphon

Emesa
Homs

Palmyra

Phoenicia

N

Mare Internum
Mediterranean Sea

Palaestina

Bostra

0   400 kms
0   250 miles

Hierosolyma ○
Jerusalem

Alexandria ○

Aegyptus

269–70

Cyrenaica

269–70 ◆
Zenobia invades Egypt

Nile

Arabia

Below: *the colonnaded main
street of Palmyra was built in
the 2nd century AD with the
profits from its extensive
trade with the East.*

2/The City of Palmyra

*The oasis city of Palmyra
in the Syrian desert became
an important centre on the
long-distance trade routes
leading to the populous
cities of the East
Mediterranean. The
Palmyrenes grew wealthy
on the profits of this trade
and adorned their city with
temples and colonnades. At
the heart of the city was the
great sanctuary of Bel, an
enormous temple standing
within a great rectangular
enclosure.*

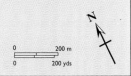

V: Restoration and Fall

The later 3rd century was marked by a programme of recovery and consolidation begun in the 270s but brought to fruition in the reign of the Emperor Diocletian. The following decades were marked by the firm government of Diocletian's colleagues and successors, culminating in the reign of Constantine, the first Christian emperor. Thereafter, though paganism lived on, Christianity was the official religion of the Roman Empire, and remained so during the declining years of Roman rule, until the abdication of the last western emperor in 476.

The Roman world of the 4th century was very different from the empire of the Julio-Claudians three hundred years before. Despite the modest eastern conquests of Diocletian, Constantine's victories north of the Danube, and Julian's ambitious Persian campaign, the Roman Empire was now very much embattled against foreign enemies. Furthermore from the middle of the 4th century, and definitively from 395, it was divided into two halves, each of which went its separate way.

Defence of the Realm

When Diocletian came to power in 284 it must have seemed that he was just another Illyrian army officer who would rule for a few years and then be murdered by the troops to make way for a successor. This had been the pattern for the past 30 years. Even an emperor as strong and successful as Aurelian had fallen victim to assassination. Yet Diocletian proved himself equal to the situation, establishing a position of power which he held for over 20 years until yielding not to murder, or even a natural death, but voluntarily abdicating to spend his last years in peaceful retirement. Given the turbulence of recent decades, this was a remarkable achievement.

On his accession Diocletian was faced by two major security concerns: the security of the empire and its frontiers; and the security of the imperial office itself. The security of the empire he addressed by increasing the size of the army. Many new legions were created, but though these were still the well-drilled infantry units familiar from earlier periods they were often substantially smaller, some of them composed of only around 1000 men, as opposed to the earlier 5000. But the army as a whole was larger than it had been in the 2nd century, and perhaps numbered as many as 400,000 men, an increase of a third. In addition, Diocletian spent much effort and outlay on the strengthening of the frontier defences.

These measures must have placed considerable strain on the resources of the state, and Diocletian accompanied them by tax reforms which sought to ensure that the army was regularly paid and adequately supplied. These new taxes were paid partly in coin, but partly in kind, itself a reflection of the decline of the monetary economy which was a hallmark of the late Roman period.

Right: *this* missorium, *or silver dish, shows the Emperor Theodosius (r. 379–95) in all the majesty with which the 4th-century rulers of Rome sought to buttress their power. The realism of earlier Imperial portraiture has given way to a remote, icon-like depiction, with more emphasis on the trappings of power—the robes and diadem—than on the physical appearance of the individual emperor.*

The Expression of Power

The frequent imperial assassinations had been a destabilizing factor during the 3rd century. Diocletian sought to counter this by introducing elaborate court ceremonial, which made the emperor remote and aloof. Henceforth, when emperors appeared in public on state occasions, they wore a jewelled diadem, jewelled shoes, and robes of purple and gold. Subjects who wished to approach them had to prostrate themselves at their feet and kiss the hem of their robe. Gone were the days when the emperor was simply *princeps* or "first citizen". That had always been something of a fiction, but now the emperor cast off all pretence and became *dominus et deus*, "lord and god". Gone also were the days when the emperor pretended to rule in consultation with the Senate; he was now absolute monarch, with a council of advisers appointed by himself.

Imperial security was improved still further by changes in the organization of the empire. Many of the rebellions of the previous half century had been made possible by the fact that a provincial governor in an important frontier province had both civil and military forces at his command. This combination made it possible for him to defy central government with little local opposition. Diocletian changed all that by separating civil and military authority. The commanders of the army no longer had civilian functions as well; each province had both a civil governor and a military commander or '*dux*'. The boundaries of the provinces had been redrawn once before by Septimius Severus. Now the Severan provinces were yet further subdivided, so that provincial governors controlled smaller territories and had even less individual power. Britain, for instance, which had originally been a single province, was divided into two by Severus, and into four by Diocletian. The provinces in turn were grouped into 12 larger units, or dioceses, controlled by "vicars" directly responsible to the imperial administration.

The most radical change in the position of emperor was Diocletian's co-option of colleagues. This arose from the recognition that the problems facing the empire (and especially the frontier threats) were too great to be handled by one ruler alone. Diocletian appointed his first colleague, Maximian, as "Caesar" (junior emperor) in 285, and promoted him to "Augustus" (senior emperor, on an equal footing with himself) a year later. In 293, the number of emperors was increased to four by the appointment of junior emperors in both west and east. This division of power—known as the tetrarchy—had important consequences for the future. It institutionalized the distinction between eastern and western halves of the empire, which was to become more firmly fixed in the course of the 4th century, and was to lead after 395 to a situation where the two halves operated independently of each other.

Constantine and Christianity

Diocletian's reforms set the pattern of imperial administration for decades to come. The tetrarchy itself, however, soon fell victim to individual ambition. When Diocletian abdicated in 305 he forced his senior colleague Maximian to do so also, and together they passed on the mantle of government to their junior colleagues Constantius and Galerius, who became the new senior emperors. They in turn appointed new junior colleagues, so that the tetrarchic arrangement was continued. When Constantius died in 306, however, cracks began to show. His son, Constantine, was recognized by the

Right: *the Basilica Nova was begun by Maxentius, who seized power at Rome in 306, but only completed after Constantine's victory at the Milvian bridge brought the city under his control.*

Diocletian's Edict on Maximum Prices, 301

In 301 the Emperor Diocletian published this edict in an attempt to check inflation, which he attributed to "unlimited and frenzied avarice". Prices are given in *denarii*, but by this period the *denarius* was merely an accounting unit, and not represented by a physical coin. Its relationship to the actual coins struck by Diocletian and his successors is still not understood.

I:		*denarii*
wheat	1 army *modius**	100
barley	1 army *modius*	60
rye	1 army *modius*	60
...		
lentils	1 army *modius*	100
...		

II. Likewise, for wines:

Picene	1 Italian *sextarius*	30
Tiburtine	1 Italian *sextarius*	30
...		
ordinary	1 Italian *sextarius*	8
...		
beer, Gallic or Pannonian	1 Italian *sextarius*	4
beer, Egyptian	1 Italian *sextarius*	4

III. Likewise, for oil:

from unripe olives	1 Italian *sextarius*	40
second quality	1 Italian *sextarius*	24
...		

IV. Likewise, for meat:

pork	1 Italian pound	12
beef	1 Italian pound	8
...		

V. Likewise, for fish:

sea fish	1 Italian pound	24
fish, second quality	1 Italian pound	16
river fish, best quality	1 Italian pound	12
river fish, second quality	1 Italian pound	8
oysters	100	100

VII. For wages:

farm labourer, with maintenance	daily	25
carpenter, as above	daily	50
wall painter, as above	daily	75
picture painter, as above	daily	150
baker, as above	daily	50
...		
elementary teacher, per boy	monthly	75
...		
check-room attendant per bather	daily	2

* a standard sized container used for dry goods.

western provinces as his father's successor, but only grudgingly accepted by the other tetrarchs. At about the same time Maxentius, son of Diocletian's colleague Maximian, declared himself emperor at Rome, and took possession of Italy and North Africa. The consequence was a series of civil wars and political settlements which ended only with the overthrow of the tetrarchy and the victory of Constantine as sole ruler in 324.

Under Constantine, the programme of administrative and military reform continued. He was responsible for dividing the Roman army into frontier troops and mobile field units, a move which was criticized by some observers since they felt it weakened the frontiers. Constantine himself was a successful military commander, however, who won not only civil wars but also campaigned successfully against Germans and Goths. But his most famous innovation was not military or administrative, it was religious: the adoption of Christianity as the official state religion.

Christians had had a bad start to the 4th century. In February 303 the eastern emperors Diocletian and

Above: an integral part of Diocletian's reforms was his restoration of a stable currency. Mints that had sprung up throughout the empire to meet the emergencies of the 3rd century were regularized, and new ones created. All struck to a standard design, and the mint's initials on the reverse allowed any lapse in quality to be traced to its source. Like the crisis money of the later 3rd century, Diocletian's coins were of bronze with a thin silver wash on the surface, but they were much larger and more carefully made. The aggressive, bull-headed portraits of Diocletian and his colleagues illustrate their military preoccupations and the need to impress their power upon the populace.

Galerius had issued an edict ordering the destruction of churches and scriptures. It was followed soon afterwards by other edicts, culminating in the command that everyone must offer sacrifice to the pagan gods. This the Christians refused to do, and they died in their thousands in consequence. The persecution continued in the eastern provinces until 312, but after the initial onslaught it became spasmodic and haphazard

Above: *this wall painting, from a villa at Lullingstone in Kent, depicts two Christians praying with outstretched hands. It dates from the mid-4th century, when a small room in the villa appears to have been converted into a chapel.*

in nature, and never had much impact in the west.

It was one thing to tolerate, another actually to adopt the Christian religion. Yet that was what Constantine did, after his victory over Maxentius at the Milvian bridge just north of Rome in October 312. He claimed to have seen a vision of the cross in the noonday sky shortly before the battle, with the divine command "Conquer by this". Whatever the truth, whether through policy or personal conviction, Constantine henceforth became a committed Christian. He took an interventionist line in the affairs of the Christian church, presiding in person at Church councils, while at the same time admitting Christian bishops to his inner circle of counsellors.

Temple treasures were confiscated and used to fund a major programme of church building, including the first St Peter's at Rome and the churches built over the Holy Places at Jerusalem and Bethlehem. Paganism did not suddenly disappear, however, and despite edicts designed to discourage or prohibit pagan practices, non-Christians continued to hold high positions at court throughout the 4th century.

One final feature of Constantine's reign was the further eclipse of Rome as a centre of imperial government. Constantine himself had at one time planned to be buried there, but in 330 he dedicated a new capital at Constantinople on the Bosphorus. This was a Christian capital, without the heavy legacy of pagan temples and institutions so conspicuous at Rome. It also illustrated an importance shift in the imperial centre of gravity, with the eastern provinces increasingly important as the west slipped into decline.

Right: *the early 6th-century church of St Sergius and Bacchus at Rasafah, an important late Roman garrison town in Syria. The west end of the church was formed by a pair of towers; at the east end, the semi-circular apse was covered by a half dome.*

The Successors of Constantine

By the time Constantine died in 337 he had divided the empire among his three surviving sons Constantine II, Constantius II and Constans. He had intended his step-brother's son Flavius Iulius Dalmatius to be a fourth Caesar, but Constantine's sons murdered him within six months. Next to go was Constantine II, killed in battle against his brother Constans in 340. Constans himself was killed fleeing from the usurper Magnentius in 350. Only Constantius survived to die a natural death, in November 360, but even he reached only 44, and he was about to do battle with his cousin Julian when he was carried off by a fever.

Constantine's sons may have had few scruples in dealing with their rivals— or indeed with each other—but they all claimed to be Christian emperors. Julian, however, was a staunch advocate of the traditional religion, and tried in various ways to turn back the clock. He removed the tax exemption which Constantine had given to Christian clergy, and renewed the practice of pagan sacrifice with great enthusiasm. He provoked Christians even further by arbitrarily closing the Great Church at Antioch and threatening to rebuild the Temple at Jerusalem as a counterpoise to Constantine's church of the Holy Sepulchre. Actions such as these unsettled even many pagan believers, but Julian did not survive to carry out all his schemes. He was killed in his ambitious but abortive Persian campaign of 363.

Above: *silver coins of the later 4th century. As part of his reform, Diocletian had reintroduced coins of fine silver, but they were never issued in very large quantities and the denomination was soon debased. It was not until the reign of Constantius II (337–61) that the empire once again had a silver coinage plentiful enough to form a regular part of the currency. The large number of silver hoards found in Britian reflects both the success of this coinage and the prosperity of the province during its last decades of Roman rule.*

Julian's successors were Christians, but it was not until the final years of the 4th century that they began to take further steps to eradicate pagan belief. In 384 the regional governor Cynegius ordered the closure of temples in Egypt. Seven years later, the Emperor Theodosius issued a series of further edicts prohibiting pagan sacrifice and withdrawing subsidies from pagan priests. The strength of feeling against pagans drove groups of Christians—even monks—to attack pagan temples and synagogues. Christianity was so powerful that a prominent bishop such as Ambrose of Milan could even impose humiliating public penance on the Emperor Theodosius himself.

For the ordinary people, those working the land, the 4th century was a time of increasing repression. A law of 332 tied tenant farmers to the land, to prevent them avoiding payment of poll tax. This was one of many examples of the growing authoritarianism of the late empire. Another trend was the increasing wealth of the very rich, at the very same time as the poor were suffering taxation and oppression. Wealthy landowners amassed enormous estates and lived on them in palatial villas surrounded by storerooms and workshops which could take on the character of small towns. While some regions of the empire were in economic difficulty, others, such as Syria and North Africa, experienced renewed prosperity as the century drew to its close.

Knowledge of the official administrative and military structure at this period comes to us from a 1551 copy of an official 4th-century document, the *Notitia Dignitatum* ("list of offices"), which details the civil and military commands of the empire and preserves the name and even the insignia of individual military units. It also lists the imperial factories established by Diocletian to supply the army with weapons and other materials.

The Gothic Invasions

In military terms, the last decades of the 4th century were dominated by the menace of the Goths. This Germanic people had settled north of the Black Sea and had already raided Asia Minor and the Balkan provinces of the Roman empire during the middle decades of the 3rd century. By the later 4th century the Goths found themselves under considerable pressure from a new nomadic enemy, the Huns, on their eastern flank, and sought refuge within the territories of the empire. Valens, the eastern emperor, allowed one group to enter, but later so badly maltreated them that they rebelled. In a great battle fought at Adrianople in 378 the army of the eastern empire suffered a crushing defeat, and Valens himself was killed.

By this time the empire was definitively divided into two halves, east and west. The division took its final form when Valentinian I (364–75) gave control of the east to his brother Valens (364–78). Yet in 378, in this moment of crisis for the eastern empire, authority reverted to Valentinian's son and successor in the west, the Emperor Gratian (367–83). He installed his army commander Theodosius I as the new eastern emperor. To Theodosius fell the enormous task of clearing the Goths from the Balkans, or at least bringing them under control. This was achieved only by allowing them to settle within the empire under their own king, normally as an ally of Rome but effectively as an armed and autonomous people.

The Sack of Rome

When Theodosius died in 395 his young sons Arcadius and Honorius were installed as respectively eastern and western emperors. The Goths chose this moment to break into open rebellion. Under their new leader Alaric they advanced on Constantinople and then embarked on an orgy of killing and looting in Greece. The year 397 found them in Epirus (northwest Greece), and there they settled for four years until in 401 they made a first invasion of Italy. That was turned back by Stilicho, the army commander appointed by Theodosius to take care of Honorius. A second invasion in 407 was bought off. They were back the following year, however, and in 410, after two years seeking to negotiate with the vacillating government of Honorius, they lost patience and sacked Rome.

The event was regarded as a catastrophe by contemporaries, even though Rome was no longer the seat of imperial government in Italy; that had been moved to Ravenna, safe behind its coastal marshes. The western empire was indeed already in crisis, beset not only by Goths but by rival emperors and by armies of Vandals, Alans and Suebi who had crossed the Rhine and were ravaging Gaul. The Goths themselves left Italy and were eventually ceded a kingdom centred on Toulouse in 418. Honorius survived five more years, dying of disease in 423. By that time, Britain, together with large areas of Gaul and Spain, were effectively beyond his control.

Honorius's successors in the west fared little better. The long reign of Valentinian III (423–55) saw the defeat of the Hunnish leader Attila at the battle of the Catalaunian Fields in 453, but failed to turned back the trend to fragmentation. North Africa fell to the Vandals in 439. The western emperors who followed Valentinian gradually yielded more and more power to the Germanic commanders who controlled their armies, eventually becoming little more than figureheads. The last of all, Romulus Augustus (known dismissively as Augustulus, "the little Augustus"), abdicated in 476, withdrawing with a comfortable pension to Campania.

The abdication of Romulus Augustus marks the end of the Roman empire in the west, which henceforth was a mosaic of Germanic kingdoms ruled by Ostrogoths, Visigoths, Vandals, Franks, Saxons and others. Within these territories, the Roman aristocracy survived, reading and writing in Latin as before (only in Britain was Latin displaced), and putting their administrative skills to the service of new masters. In the east, by contrast, the Roman empire remained strong. Its emperors frequently intervened in western affairs; the most powerful of them, Justinian I (527–65), actually reconquered a substantial part of the lost western provinces. Much of this territory was lost again in the century that followed, but the Byzantine realm survived, its Greek-speaking rulers continuing to style themselves "Emperor of the Romans" until the last of them died by the city walls when the Ottoman Turks conquered Constantinople in 1453.

Right: the Germanic peoples who invaded the Roman Empire in the 5th century did not set out to overthrow it, but to share in its wealth. This late 5th- or 6th-century mosaic from Carthage depicts a Vandal lord who has successfully acquired the trappings of Roman life, including a comfortable villa in the lush North African farmland.

Diocletian and the Division of Power

The accession of Diocletian in 284 brought an end to 50 years of imperial decline and ushered in a period of reorganization and recovery.

One of Diocletian's first acts was to name a colleague, Maximian, as emperor with responsibility for the western provinces. That was in 285. Eight years later the division of power was taken a stage further when Diocletian and Maximian each appointed a junior colleague: Galerius in the east, Constantius (father of Constantine) in the west. Thus was established the tetrarchy, the system of government which divided overall responsibility between a college of four regional emperors, headed by Diocletian. Rome was abandoned as a major imperial residence, and new centres established nearer the troubled frontiers: Trier and Milan, Thessalonica and Nicomedia.

Diocletian's reorganization of the imperial administration went much further than a simple division of power—he comprehensively overhauled the provinces, creating a system of smaller provinces grouped into 12 larger administrative units called dioceses. Another crucial innovation was the separation of civil and military power; governors of provinces and dioceses had no military authority and army commands were organized in a way which cross-cut provincial boundaries. The aim was to remove once and for all the threat of insurrection by powerful provincial governors.

Above: the four tetrarchs embrace, swords at the ready, symbolizing their union in defence of the empire. This marble sculpture, dating from c. 300, was later set into the angle of St Mark's basilica in Venice.

Diocletian also addressed the empire's economic problems, increasing the weight of the gold coins, issuing the first good silver for a century and reorganizing the mints. A uniform coinage was struck throughout the empire, and each coin carried the name of the mint which produced it so that any lapse in quality could be traced to its source. In 301 he attempted to curb inflation by freezing of wages and prices, but this did not hold for long. On the whole, however, Diocletian's reforms were so successful that in 305 he was able to abdicate voluntarily.

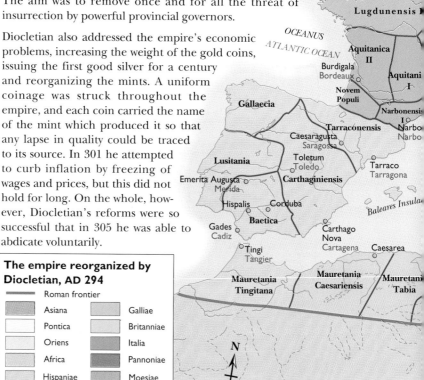

Britannia II

Flavia Caesariensis

Britannia I

Londini
London

Maxima Caesariensis

principal ◆
residence of
Constantius

Belg
I

Lugdunensis

OCEANUS
ATLANTIC OCEAN

Aquitanica
II

Burdigala
Bordeaux

Aquitani
I

Novem
Populi

Gallaecia

Narbonensis
I
Narbo
Narbo

Tarraconensis

Caesaragusta
Saragossa

Lusitania

Toletum
Toledo

Tarraco
Tarragona

Emerita Augusta
Merida

Carthaginiensis

Hispalis   Corduba

Baleares Insulae

Baetica

Gades
Cadiz

Carthago
Nova
Cartagena   Caesarea

Tingi
Tangier

Mauretania
Tingitana

Mauretania
Caesariensis

Mauretani
Tabia

The empire reorganized by Diocletian, AD 294

	Roman frontier		
	Asiana		Galliae
	Pontica		Britanniae
	Oriens		Italia
	Africa		Pannoniae
	Hispaniae		Moesiae
	Viennensis		Thraciae
🏛	Imperial residence	●	mint

N

| 0 | 450 kms |
| 0 | 300 miles |

Right: *the only Roman emperor to abdicate voluntarily, Diocletian built himself this vast villa at Split. The colonnaded peristyle, or courtyard, led to the mausoleum in which Diocletian was eventually interred.*

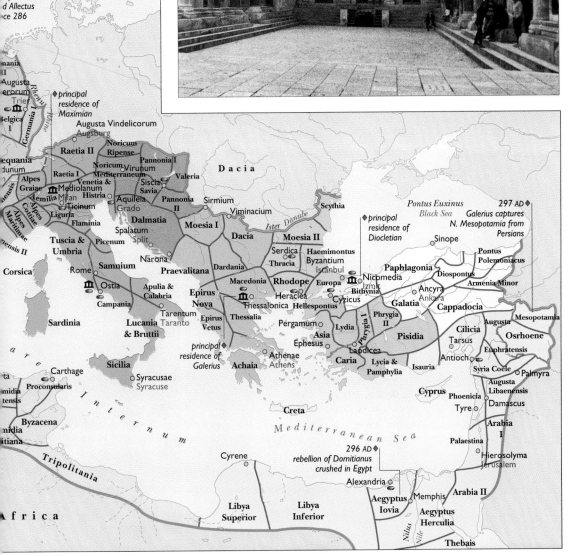

297 AD
nstantius restores
man rule to
tain, ruled by
urpers Carausius
d Allectus
ce 286

♦ *principal residence of Maximian*

Augusta Vindelicorum
Augsburg

Noricum
Ripense

Raetia II

Pannonia I

Noricum
Mediterraneum Virunum

Raetia I

Venetia &
Histria

Valeria

Siscia
Savia

D a c i a

Mediolanum
Milan

Aemilia

Alpes
Graiae

Alpes
Cottiae

Ticinum

Liguria

Aquileia
Grado

Pannonia
II

Sirmium

Scythia

Pontus Euxinus
Black Sea

297 AD ♦

Galerius captures
N. Mesopotamia from
Persians

Flaminia

Dalmatia
Spalatum
Split

Viminacium

Moesia I

Dacia

Ister Danube

Moesia II

♦ *principal residence of Diocletian*

Sinope

Pontus
Polemoniacus

Tuscia &
Umbria

Picenum

Narona

Praevalitana

Dardania

Serdica
Thracia

Haemimontus
Byzantium
Istanbul

Paphlagonia

Diospontus

Armenia Minor

Corsica

Rome

Samnium

Ostia

Apulia &
Calabria

Epirus
Nova

Macedonia

Rhodope

Europa

Heraclea

Thessalonica Hellespontus

Nicomedia
Izmit
Bithynia

Cyzicus

Ancyra
Ankara

Galatia

Cappadocia

Augusta

Mesopotamia

Campania

Tarentum
Taranto

Epirus
Vetus

Thessalia

Pergamum

Phrygia I

Phrygia
II

Pisidia

Cilicia
Tarsus

Osrhoene

Sardinia

Lucania
& Bruttii

principal residence of Galerius ♦

Achaia

Athenae
Athens

Asia

Ephesus

Lydia

Caria

Laodicea

Lycia &
Pamphylia

Isauria

Antioch

Syria Coele

Euphratensis

Palmyra

Cyprus

Phoenicia

Augusta
Libaenensis

Damascus

a r e

Carthage

Sicilia

Syracusae
Syracuse

Creta

Tyre

Arabia
I

ta

Proconsularis

idia
tensis

I n t e r n u m

M e d i t e r r a n e a n   S e a

Palaestina

Byzacena

nidia
itiana

u m

296 AD ♦

rebellion of Domitianus crushed in Egypt

Hierosolyma
Jerusalem

Tripolitania

Cyrene

Alexandria

Arabia II

A f r i c a

Libya
Superior

Libya
Inferior

Aegyptus
Iovia

Memphis

Aegyptus
Herculia

Nilus Nile

Thebais

Germania I
Augusta
erorum
Trier

Belgica
I

equania
dunum

Alpes
Maritimae

ensis II

nania
I

The Spread of Christianity

Christianity first took hold in the east, but apart from an early appearance at Rome itself, it did not become popular in the west until the 3rd century.

For many years, Christianity was just one of a number of oriental religions gaining adherents in the major cities of the Roman Empire (▶ *page 102–3*). It first achieved official notoriety in the reign of Nero, who made the Christians the scapegoats for the Great Fire of Rome in AD 64. The historical Jesus had died some 35 years before, but Christianity spread quickly through the eastern provinces, and by the 50s there was even a Christian community at Rome.

By the end of the 1st century, the pattern of toleration alternating with persecution, which was to continue until the reign of Constantine in the early 4th century, had been established. Domitian (AD 81–96), like Nero, is said to have persecuted Christians; "good" emperors such as Trajan (AD 98–117) chose to ignore them as far as possible. The serious persecutions began in the 3rd century, when Christianity was well established even among the ruling classes, but came to be seen as a threat to the state. In 250 the Emperor Decius (AD 249– 51) issued an edict requiring all citizens of the empire to make sacrifice to the traditional gods of Rome. Unable to do this, many Christians suffered torture and death.

Persecution was renewed in 303 in a last-ditch attempt by Galerius to bolster the old faith, but in 312 the Emperor Constantine made Christianity the state religion; he was baptized on his deathbed in 337. Paganism was still tolerated, but temple treasures were confiscated and used to support a major church-building programme. This included the first St Peter's in Rome and churches over the holy places of Bethlehem and Jerusalem, where Constantine's mother Helena claimed to have found the cross on which Christ was crucified. Constantine took a personal interest in Christian doctrine, and supervised the church councils at Arles and Nicaea to combat heresy. The link between church and state was to remain a powerful force for centuries to come.

"With them were four women. Ammonarion, a most respectable young woman, in spite of the savage and prolonged torture… kept true to her promise and was led away. The others were Mercuria, a very dignified lady, and Dionysia, the mother of a large family but just as devoted to her Lord. The governor was ashamed to go on torturing without results and to be defeated by women, so they died by the sword without being put to any further test by torture…"

The persecution of Christians under Decius (AD 250), from Eusebius, *Ecclesiastical History*

OCEANUS ATLANTIC OCEAN

Burdigala
Bordeaux

Caesaraugusta
Saragossa

Toletum
Toledo

Corduba

Illiberis
Elvira
306

Cartha
Nova
Cartage

N

0   450 kms
0   300 miles

Right: *early Christian communities at Rome excavated large communal cemeteries (catacombs) outside the city boundaries for the burial of their dead. These were not places of worship, though memorial services were sometimes held there. The Chapel of the Popes, in the Catacomb of S. Callisto, was built around AD 250.*

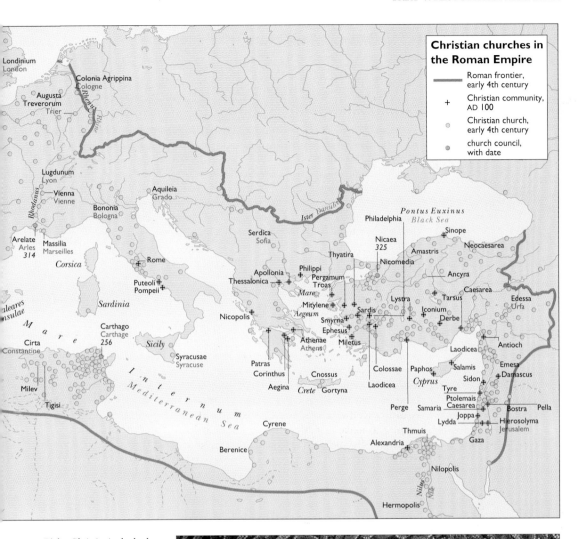

Christian churches in the Roman Empire

- Roman frontier, early 4th century
- + Christian community, AD 100
- Christian church, early 4th century
- church council, with date

Londinium London
Colonia Agrippina Cologne
Augusta Treverorum Trier
Lugdunum Lyon
Vienna Vienne
Bononia Bologna
Aquileia Grado
Arelate Arles 314
Massilia Marseilles
Corsica
Rome
Puteoli *Pompeii*
Sardinia
Carthago Carthage 256
Sicily
Syracusae Syracuse
Cirta Constantine
Milev
Tigisi
Serdica Sofia
Thyatira
Nicaea 325
Nicomedia
Amastris
Neocaesarea
Sinope
Philadelphia
Pontus Euxinus Black Sea
Apollonia
Thessalonica
Philippi
Pergamum *Troas*
Ancyra
Mare Aegeum
Mitylene
Smyrna
Ephesus
Sardis
Lystra
Tarsus
Iconium
Derbe
Caesarea
Edessa Urfa
Nicopolis
Athenae Athens
Miletus
Antioch
Laodicea
Emesa
Damascus
Patras *Corinthus*
Cnossus
Colossae
Paphos
Salamis
Cyprus
Sidon
Tyre
Aegina
Crete *Gortyna*
Laodicea
Perge
Samaria
Ptolemais *Caesarea*
Bostra
Pella
Joppa
Lydda
Hierosolyma Jerusalem
Cyrene
Thmuis
Gaza
Berenice
Alexandria
Nilopolis
Hermopolis
Nilus Nile
Internum Mediterranean Sea
Ister Danube
Rhodanus
Baleares Insulae

Right: *Christianity had taken root in Britain by the early 4th century, when this mosaic was installed in a Roman villa at Hinton St Mary in Dorset. The image is clearly identified as Christ by the Chi-Rho monogram—the first letters of the Greek Chrestos, Christ—while the pomegranates symbolize eternal life.*

Constantine the Great

Above: *this carved plinth supports an obelisk brought from Egypt and set up in the Hippodrome at Constantinople. It shows the Emperor Theodosius I (379–95), surrounded by his family and courtiers, watching the races from the imperial box.*

Unwilling to share power, Constantine defeated his rivals and reunified the empire, giving it a new religion and a new capital.

The system of divided rule which Diocletian had established did not long survive his retirement in 305. In the west, the struggle was between Maxentius, who had seized Italy and North Africa, and Constantine, who had succeeded his father Constantius as western emperor in 306. In 312 Constantine invaded Italy and defeated Maxentius at Turin and Verona, then at the battle of the Milvian Bridge. This left him undisputed ruler of the western provinces. Constantine at first agreed a division of power with Licinius, who controlled the east, but by 316 he felt strong enough to attack his rival, seizing Greece and the Balkans. The ensuing truce lasted until 324, when Constantine finally defeated Licinius; his victory reunited the Roman Empire under the rule of one man.

Constantine used his power to promote the religion he had adopted—Christianity. He claimed to have seen a vision of the cross of Christ the evening before the battle of the Milvian Bridge, and to have won his victory through the power of that symbol. He made Christianity the state religion, confiscating temple

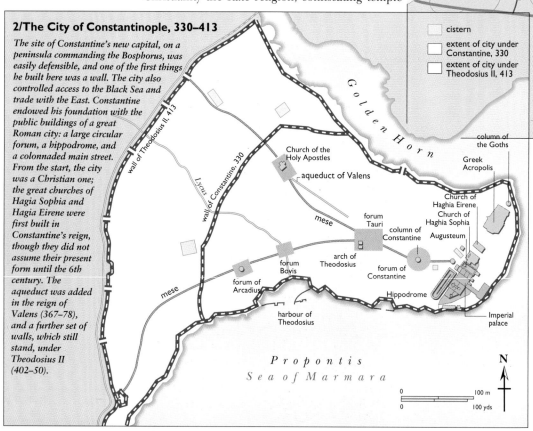

2/The City of Constantinople, 330–413

The site of Constantine's new capital, on a peninsula commanding the Bosphorus, was easily defensible, and one of the first things he built here was a wall. The city also controlled access to the Black Sea and trade with the East. Constantine endowed his foundation with the public buildings of a great Roman city: a large circular forum, a hippodrome, and a colonnaded main street. From the start, the city was a Christian one; the great churches of Hagia Sophia and Hagia Eirene were first built in Constantine's reign, though they did not assume their present form until the 6th century. The aqueduct was added in the reign of Valens (367–78), and a further set of walls, which still stand, under Theodosius II (402–50).

cistern

extent of city under Constantine, 330

extent of city under Theodosius II, 413

wall of Theodosius II, 413
wall of Constantine, 330
Lycus
Church of the Holy Apostles
aqueduct of Valens
column of the Goths
Greek Acropolis
Church of Haghia Eirene
Church of Haghia Sophia
mese
forum Tauri
column of Constantine
Augusteum
mese
forum Bovis
arch of Theodosius
forum of Arcadius
forum of Constantine
Hippodrome
harbour of Theodosius
Imperial palace

Golden Horn

*Propontis
Sea of Marmara*

N

| 0 | 100 m |
| 0 | 100 yds |

Burdig
Bordea

Caesaragusta
Saragossa

H i s p a n i a e

Emerita Augusta
Merida
Toletum
Toledo

Hispalis
Seville
Gades
Cadiz
Corduba
Cartha
Nova
Cartag
Tingi
Tangier

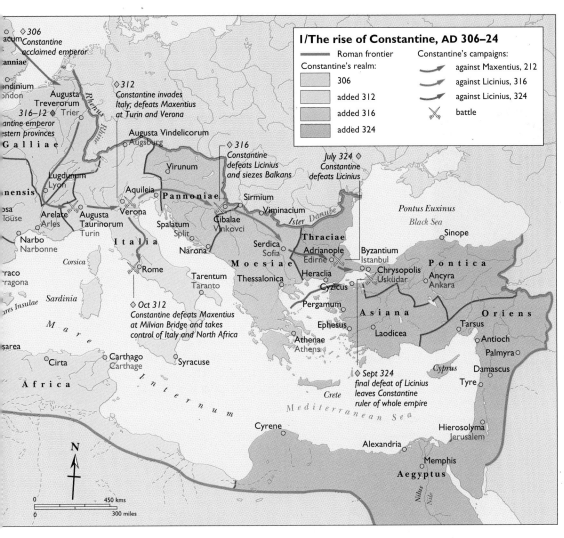

I/The rise of Constantine, AD 306–24

Roman frontier

Constantine's realm:
- 306
- added 312
- added 316
- added 324

Constantine's campaigns:
- against Maxentius, 212
- against Licinius, 316
- against Licinius, 324
- battle

Right this head of Constantine was part of a colossal statue of the emperor set up at Rome. Its massive scale and brutal simplicity reflect the changing conception of imperial power in the 4th century, as lip-service to republican form gave way to divinely-appointed autocracy.

treasures and building many new churches. He also took a personal interest in theology, participating in Church councils at Arles in 314 and Nicaea in 325, and being baptized on his deathbed in 337. Constantine strengthened the security of the empire, especially along the Danube (▶ *pages 86–87*), and reformed the army, making a distinction between frontier units and a mobile field army. He was also a lavish builder: at Trier, his first capital, and at Rome, where he built baths and completed the massive Basilica Nova whose ruins still dominate the Forum. The senate also voted him the famous Arch of Constantine, to commemorate his victory over Maxentius. One of Constantine's most lasting achievements was the transformation of the Greek city of Byzantium into a new capital, Constantinople, in 330.

Roman Technology and Engineering

Roman technical skills were applied to large-scale projects— roads, aqueducts and mines—and to everyday manufactured goods.

The empire depended for its communications on the network of all-weather roads which began as a series of strategic arteries in Italy enabling troops and supplies to be moved rapidly from one sector to another. The actual method of construction varied greatly from place to place, depending on the availability of materials and the local subsoil. In marshland, the road might take the form of a gravel causeway on a timber raft. In the eastern provinces, roads consisted of loose stone fill between carefully laid kerbs. The finest roads of all, however, were those such as the famous Via Appia, with a surface of polygonal paving slabs carefully fitted together.

The laying-out of Roman roads was in the hands of trained surveyors, as was the still more demanding discipline of aqueducts. Roman aqueducts were designed to bring drinking water from distant sources to supplement local supplies. Generally they ran in covered channels at ground level, following the natural contours; this in itself demanded skilled surveying. It is where defiles were to be crossed, however, that aqueducts became most impressive, striding on arches across a river valley or lowland plain so as to maintain the gradient of flow within the specified parameters.

For motive power, the Romans made use of wind, water, and muscle, both human and animal. Wind power was little used save for sailing ships; windmills for grinding grain were a medieval innovation. Water, however, was used for milling, both in small-scale establishments such as those at river crossings on Hadrian's Wall, and in the batteries of water mills on the hillside at Barbégal in southern France, designed to produce flour on an industrial scale. Muscle power was a more traditional source of energy. Animals

Above: glassware was widely produced throughout the empire and ranged from ornate decorative pieces to simple household containers such as this small late Roman glass bottle of the type used for cosmetics or medicines.

Right: pottery oil lamps, widely used for lighting throughout the Roman world, represent an early form of mass production; clay was pressed into stone moulds to form the upper and lower halves, which were then fixed together and fired. Many lamps could thus be produced to the same design. This small lamp, its nozzle still stained with soot, comes from Roman Egypt.

Right: many types of kiln were used to fire a wide range of pottery in the provinces of the empire. This Colchester-type kiln was widely used in Britain. The vaulted combustion chambers were sunk into the ground and lined with brick or stone. Above them, a ventilated clay floor supported the pots. The domed turf roof would have been built afresh over each new batch of pots.

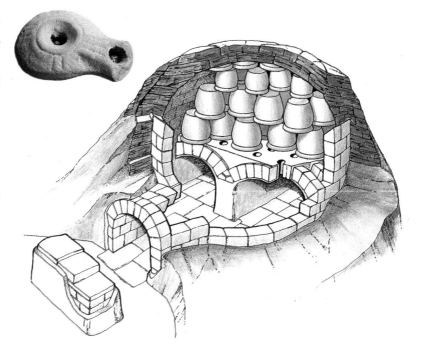

turned the rotary mills at Roman Pompeii, and the widespread availability of slave labour may have removed much of the incentive for the adoption of labour-saving devices such as the primitive steam turbine described by Hero of Alexandria.

Another dimension of engineering skill was the sinking of mines, notably for valuable metals such as copper and lead. The mines of the Iberian peninsula were especially productive, and have yielded rare examples of the technology used by the Romans to drain water from the deeper galleries, including screw pumps and water wheels.

Alongside these major engineering works the Romans also developed considerable technical skill in the manufacture of smaller items such as pottery and glassware. Some of their glassware was of remarkable quality—the Portland Vase is a fine example—but the Romans used glass even for everyday objects such as bottles. Pottery was also produced in quantity, notably the many types of *amphorae* (often locally made) or the red-slipped table wares of Gaul and North Africa. Kiln sites throughout the Roman world show that Roman potters could achieve high temperatures in carefully controlled conditions, and the ubiquity of their products is evidence of both their skill and success.

Right: *Roman mining operations sometimes used sophisticated pumping equipment to clear the lower levels of water. This series of eight pairs of water wheels was found in the Roman copper mines at Rio Tinto in Lusitania.*

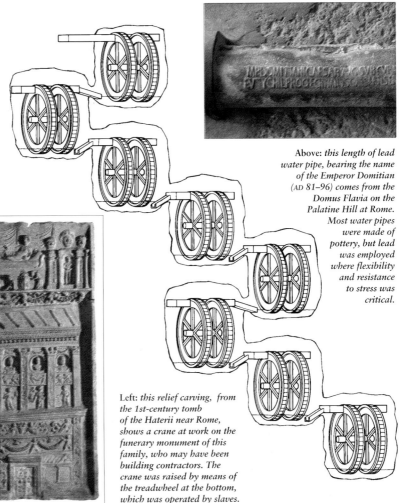

Above: *this length of lead water pipe, bearing the name of the Emperor Domitian (AD 81–96) comes from the Domus Flavia on the Palatine Hill at Rome. Most water pipes were made of pottery, but lead was employed where flexibility and resistance to stress was critical.*

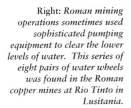

Left: *this relief carving, from the 1st-century tomb of the Haterii near Rome, shows a crane at work on the funerary monument of this family, who may have been building contractors. The crane was raised by means of the treadwheel at the bottom, which was operated by slaves.*

A Fragile Prosperity

After the troubles of the 3rd century, the 4th was a period of renewed prosperity in many parts of the Roman empire.

The reforms of Diocletian and Constantine provided a sound administrative and military structure, though they also placed a heavy tax burden on the poorer citizens. In the western provinces, the greatest prosperity was found in rural villas. The towns, by contrast, were in decline, and it seems that wealthy landowners abandoned their city houses to live on their country estates. The military threat on the Rhine–Danube frontier and in the east remained a constant menace throughout the century, and much of central government revenue was devoted to army pay and to state factories set up to supply the soldiers with weapons and clothing. The main centres of government, too, followed the Rhine–Danube axis, though were not so close to the frontier as to be directly exposed to foreign attack: Trier and Milan (later Ravenna) in the west, Sirmium and Constantinople in the east.

The best historical evidence comes from the middle of the century, from the short reign of the Emperor Julian. Between 356 and 360 he fought against Franks and Alamanni in eastern Gaul, restoring and strengthening the Rhine frontier; but many of his gains there were squandered when he withdrew troops for the abortive Persian campaign of 363, in which he was killed. Julian's most famous exploit, however, was his attempt to turn back the clock and restore the worship of the old pagan gods. He failed, and Christian bishops continued to exercise great power in the later decades of the century.

Below: several items from a massive hoard of late Roman tableware, jewellery and coins found at Hoxne in Suffolk in 1992. They include a silver pepper-pot in the form of an empress; a bangle with the woman's name Juliana; and two necklaces, one with a pendant made from a gold coin of the Emperor Gratian (r. AD 375–83). The hoard was buried some time after 407, possibly because of troubles arising from the collapse of Roman authority in Britain. Such rich hoards illustrate the luxury still available, in the hands of an élite few, during the last years of Roman rule.

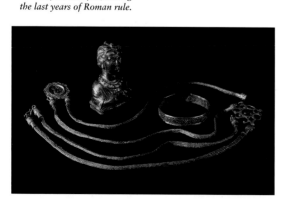

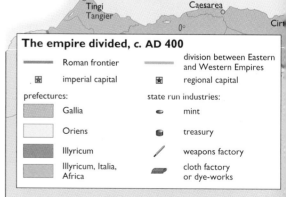

BRITANNIAE
Londinium
London

GALLIAE

Burdigala
Bordeaux

Lugdunum
Lyon

VIENNENSIS
Arelate
Arles
Narbo
Narbonne

Massil
Marseille

Salamantica
Salamanca

HISPANIAE

Tarraco
Tarragona

Emerita Augusta
Merida

Corduba

Baleares

Gades
Cadiz

Carthago Nova
Cartagena

Tingi
Tangier

Caesarea

Cirt

0°

The empire divided, c. AD 400

Roman frontier	division between Eastern and Western Empires
imperial capital	regional capital

prefectures:

- Gallia
- Oriens
- Illyricum
- Illyricum, Italia, Africa

state run industries:

- mint
- treasury
- weapons factory
- cloth factory or dye-works

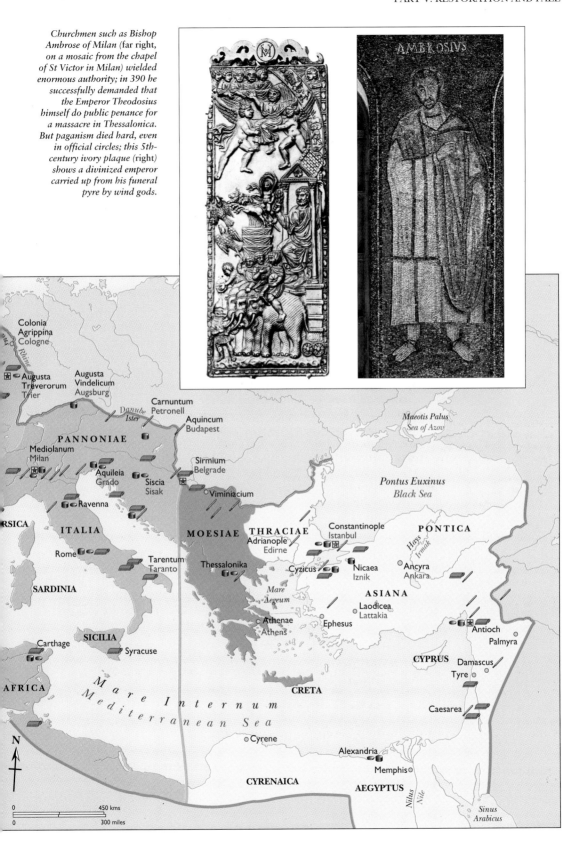

Churchmen such as Bishop Ambrose of Milan (far right, on a mosaic from the chapel of St Victor in Milan) wielded enormous authority; in 390 he successfully demanded that the Emperor Theodosius himself do public penance for a massacre in Thessalonica. But paganism died hard, even in official circles; this 5th-century ivory plaque (right) shows a divinized emperor carried up from his funeral pyre by wind gods.

The Fall of the Western Empire

The catastrophic Battle of Adrianople set in motion a chain of events which culminated in the sack of Rome.

"All the devastation, the butchery, the plundering ... which accompanied the recent disaster at Rome were in accordance with the general practice of warfare. But there was something which ... changed the whole aspect of the scene; the savagery of the barbarians took on such an aspect that the largest churches were ... set aside to be filled with people to be spared ... This is to be attributed to the name of Christ and the influence of Christianity."

St Augustine, *The City of God*

In 375 the Visigoths, seeking refuge from the Huns who were invading their territory, crossed the Danube into the Roman Empire. There they were tolerated for a while, but in 378 the Eastern Emperor Valens led an army to drive them out. It was a disastrous error; at the Battle of Adrianople the emperor was killed and his army destroyed. His successor Theodosius I concluded a peace treaty in 382 which allowed the Visigoths to settle within the empire, technically as Roman allies. In 395, however, they rebelled under their new ruler Alaric. With the aim of extracting further concessions from the Romans, they began raiding the Balkans, and in 401 invaded northern Italy. The young Western Emperor Honorius and his court abandoned their usual residence at Milan for the safety of Ravenna. Stilicho, regent to Honorius and himself of Germanic origin, drove the invaders back.

The military situation in the west became critical in December 406 when new Germanic invaders, Vandals, Alans and Suebi, crossed the Rhine in force. The sacked Trier and ravaged Gaul, then crossed the Pyrenees into Spain in 409. Frustrated in his attempts to obtain satisfactory recognition from Honorius, Alaric invaded Italy once again and on 24 August 410 the Goths sacked Rome. Though it was no longer the imperial capital, the event sent shock waves through the civilized world. Alaric died later the same year and the Visigoths left Italy for Gaul and Spain in 412; Italy remained in Roman hands. The Visigoths established an independent kingdom in Aquitaine in 418, however, and large parts of Spain were in Suebic, Alan or Vandal control. By the time the Vandals crossed to Africa and captured Carthage in 439, the Western Empire was on the verge of final breakdown.

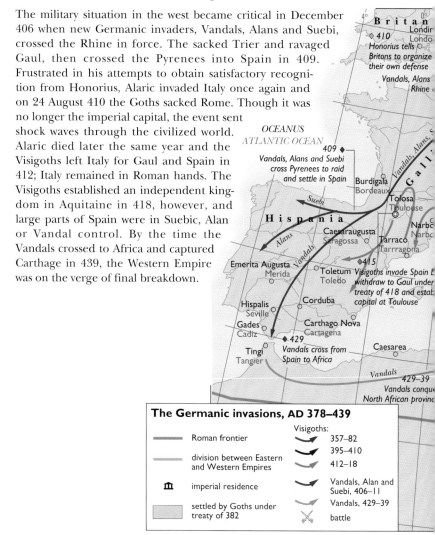

The Germanic invasions, AD 378–439

▬▬▬	Roman frontier	**Visigoths:**
		➘ 357–82
▬▬▬	division between Eastern and Western Empires	➘ 395–410
		➘ 412–18
🏛	imperial residence	➘ Vandals, Alan and Suebi, 406–11
▨	settled by Goths under treaty of 382	➘ Vandals, 429–39
		⚔ battle

Left: *Flavius Stilicho, shown here on an ebony panel, was a Vandal by birth. One of an increasing number of Germanic soldiers to achieve high rank in the Roman army, he became the effective ruler of the Western Empire after the death of Theodosius I in 395. A skilful politician, he was able to play off the Goths, the Eastern Empire and his rivals in the west against each other, but these dangerous intrigues eventually led to his fall from power and execution in 408.*

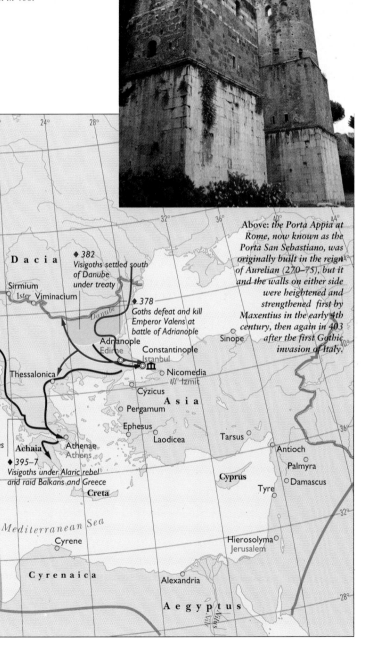

Above: *the Porta Appia at Rome, now known as the Porta San Sebastiano, was originally built in the reign of Aurelian (270–75), but it and the walls on either side were heightened and strengthened first by Maxentius in the early 4th century, then again in 403 after the first Gothic invasion of Italy.*

406 ◆ Augusta Treverorum
i cross **Trier**
ge Gaul

gdunum
on

Augusta Vindelicorum
Augsburg

◆ **402**
Western capital
moved to Ravenna

D a c i a

◆ **382**
Visigoths settled south
of Danube
under treaty

Mediolanum
Milan

Aquileia
Grado

Siscia

Sirmium
Ister Viminacium

◆ **378**
Goths defeat and kill
Emperor Valens at
battle of Adrianople

Sinope

◆ **412**
Athaulf leads
Visigoths into Gaul

Ravenna

Spalatus
Split

Narona

Danube

Adrianople
Edirne

Constantinople
Istanbul

Corsica

Rome

◆ **401–2**
Alaric's first invasion of
Italy turned back by
Stilicho

Tarentum
Taranto

Thessalonica

Nicomedia
Izmit

◆ **410**
Alaric invades Italy
a second time and
sacks Rome

Cyzicus

A s i a

Pergamum

Sardinia

◆ **439**
Carthage falls
to Vandals

Sicilia
Syracuse

◆ **410**
Alaric contemplates
invasion of Sicily
and Africa but
dies of illness

Achaia

Athenae
Athens

Ephesus

Laodicea

Tarsus

Antioch

Palmyra

ta

Carthage

◆ **395–7**
Visigoths under Alaric rebel
and raid Balkans and Greece

Creta

Cyprus

Tyre

Damascus

M a r e   I n t e r n u m

Mediterranean Sea

A
f
r
i
c
a

Cyrene

Hierosolyma
Jerusalem

Cyrenaica

Alexandria

A e g y p t u s

750 km

400 miles

The Inheritors

Above: *the mausoleum of Theodoric at Ravenna. The Ostrogothic King Theodoric ousted Odoacer in 488, with the support of the Byzantine Emperor Zeno, and ruled Italy until his death in 526.*

While Roman emperors continued to rule their eastern dominions from Constantinople, Germanic kings struggled for power in the west.

By the end of the 4th century the Roman Empire was divided into two halves, east and west, each with its own emperor. The emperors—at times openly at war—presented a disunited front to the Germanic peoples pressing on their frontiers. The west, the weaker of the two halves, was dismembered in the course of the 5th century. The Visigoths established a kingdom in Aquitaine in 418, and extended their power to Spain. Vandals raided Gaul and Spain before crossing to Africa and conquering the old Roman province by 439. Anglo-Saxons raided and settled eastern Britain during the 4th and 5th centuries, changing the language and establishing their own kingdoms. In the late 5th century France came increasingly under the control of the Franks; at Vouillé in 507 they defeated the Visigoths and advanced their borders to the Pyrenees. Italy itself became part of the

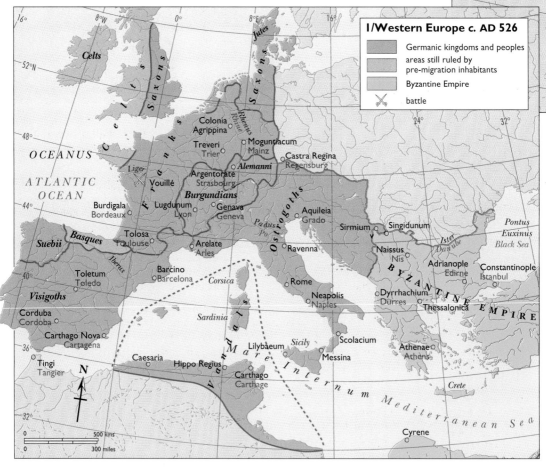

I/Western Europe c. AD 526

- Germanic kingdoms and peoples
- areas still ruled by pre-migration inhabitants
- Byzantine Empire
- ✗ battle

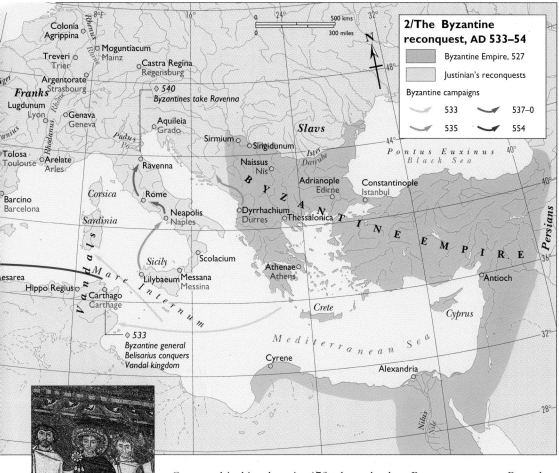

2/The Byzantine reconquest, AD 533–54

- Byzantine Empire, 527
- Justinian's reconquests

Byzantine campaigns
- 533
- 535
- 537–0
- 554

◇ 540
Byzantines take Ravenna

◇ 533
Byzantine general
Belisarius conquers
Vandal kingdom

Above: *the Emperor Justinian (r. 527–65), depicted on a mosaic in the church of San Vitale at Ravenna. The mosaic was made soon after Justinian's troops captured Ravenna in 540; the city remained the capital of the Byzantine territories in Italy until 751.*

Ostrogothic kingdom in 476 when the last Roman emperor, Romulus Augustus, was forced to abdicate and sent into comfortable retirement in Campania.

The transition from Roman province to Germanic kingdom did not mark an abrupt break with the past. In many areas the existing provincial aristocracy continued to hold land and power, to write and worship as before, only now as vassals of Germanic élites. The new rulers needed these people to run their realms. Christianity remained the dominant religion and bishops took on a growing importance, save only in eastern Britain. Here change was more radical, and the mission of Saint Augustine (597) was required to begin the conversion of the Anglo-Saxons to Christianity.

The Eastern Empire (from this time referred to as Byzantine) escaped the fate of the west, and continued to flourish under a series of capable emperors. In the first half of the 6th century, the Emperor Justinian even reconquered of some of the lost western provinces: North Africa, where the Vandal kingdom fell in 533; Italy and Sicily, where the Byzantines retained a foothold for over 200 years; and Spain. The hold on Spain proved tenuous, however, and most of Italy fell to the Lombards in 568. By the middle of the following century, Slavs in the Balkans and Arabs in the Near East and North Africa had stripped Byzantium of much of its territory. From this point, the empire was just one of several states jockeying for power in the Mediterranean world of the early Middle Ages.

Rulers of Rome, 753 BC–AD 565

ROME'S LEGENDARY KINGS

BC
753–717   ROMULUS
715–673   NUMA POMPILIUS
673–642   TULLUS HOSTILIUS
642–617   ANCUS MARTIUS
616–579   L. TARQUINIUS PRISCUS
578–535   SERVIUS TULLIUS
535–510   L. TARQUINIUS SUPERBUS

LEADING STATESMEN OF THE REPUBLIC

509   Lucius Junius BRUTUS *consul*
486   SPURIUS CASSIUS *consul*
485–79   *consulship held by patrician family the* FABII
458   Lucius Quinctius CINCINNATUS *dictator*
451–50   The Decemvirs *council of ten*
377   G. LICINIUS Stolo & Lucius SEXTIUS *consuls*
367   M. Furius CAMILLUS *dictator*
356   G. Marcus RUTILUS *first plebeian dictator*
312   APPIUS CLAUDIUS Caecus *censor*
217   Q. FABIUS MAXIMUS *dictator*
205, 194   P. Cornelius SCIPIO (AFRICANUS) *consul*
184   M. Porcius CATO *censor*
168   L. Aemilius Paulus *consul*
142   P. SCIPIO AEMILIANUS & L. MUMMIUS
           consuls
133   TIBERIUS GRACCHUS *tribune*
123–22   GAIUS GRACCHUS *tribune*
115   M. Aemilius SCAURUS *princeps senatus*
109   Q. Caecilius METELLUS *consul*
107–86   G. MARIUS *consul 7 times*
81–79   Lucius Cornelius SULLA *dictator*
66   Gn. Pompeius (POMPEY) *extraordinary powers*
63   M. Tullius CICERO *consul*
60–53   First Triumvirate:
               POMPEY; G. JULIUS CAESAR;
               M. Licinius CRASSUS
49–44   JULIUS CAESAR *dictator*
43–36   Second Triumvirate:
               G. Julius Caesar Octavianus (OCTAVIAN);
               Marcus Antonius (MARK ANTONY);
               M. Aemilius LEPIDUS
30–27   OCTAVIAN *consul with special powers*

These lists are selective: only the most important Republican statesmen are given; some junior emperors and short-lived usurpers are omitted. The name by which a person is best known to history is given in capitals. Nicknames, e.g. Caligula, and Anglicizations, e.g. Mark Antony, are placed in brackets. The Roman names Gaius and Gnaius are often spelled with a C, a survival of the time (before the 3rd century BC) when the Latin alphabet had no G. The G is used throughout this book to reflect their actual pronunciation.

EMPERORS

The Julio-Claudian Dynasty
27BC–AD14 Caesar AUGUSTUS (Octavian)
14–37   TIBERIUS Claudius Nero
37–41   Gaius Caesar Germanicus (CALIGULA)
41–54   Tiberius CLAUDIUS Nero Germanicus
54–68   NERO Claudius Caesar Drusus Germanicus
                              *
68–69   Servius Sulpicius GALBA
69   M. Salvius OTHO
69   Aulus VITELLIUS

The Flavian Dynasty
69–79   T. Flavius Vespasianus (VESPASIAN)
79–81   TITUS Flavius Vespasianus
81–96   T. Flavius Domitianus (DOMITIAN)

The Adoptive Emperors
96–98   M. Cocceius NERVA
98–117   Marcus Ulpius Traianus (TRAJAN)
117–38   P. Aelius Hadrianus (HADRIAN)
138–61   T. Aurelius Fulvus Boionius Arrius
           Antoninus (ANTONINUS PIUS)
161–80   Marcus Aelius Aurelius Verus
           (MARCUS AURELIUS)
161–9   L. Aurelius Verus (LUCIUS VERUS)
           associate emperor with Marcus Aurelius
180–92   L. Aurelius COMMODUS
                              *
193   P. Helvius PERTINAX
193   M. DIDIUS JULIANUS
193–4   G. PESCENNIUS NIGER
193–7   Decimus CLODIUS ALBINUS

The Severan Dynasty
193–211   Lucius SEPTIMIUS SEVERUS
211–17   M. Aurelius Antoninus (CARACALLA)
211–12   P. Septimius GETA
217–18   M. Opellius MACRINUS
218–22   M. Aurelius Antoninus (ELAGABALUS)
222–35   M. Aurelius SEVERUS ALEXANDER
                              *
235–8   G. Julius Verus MAXIMINUS
238–44   M. Antonius Gordianus (GORDIAN III)
244–9   M. Julius Philippus (PHILIP)
249–51   G. Messius Quintus Traianus Decius
           (TRAJAN DECIUS)
251–3   G. Vibius TREBONIANUS GALLUS
253–60   P. Licinius Valerianus (VALERIAN)
253–68   P. Licinius Egnatius GALLIENUS

Gallic Emperors
259–68   M. Cassianius Latinius POSTUMUS
268–70   M. Piavonius VICTORINUS
270–73   G. Pius Esuvius TETRICUS

The Illyrian Emperors

268–70	M. Aurelius CLAUDIUS II "GOTHICUS"
270–75	L. Domitius Aurelianus (AURELIAN)
275–76	M. Claudius TACITUS
276–82	M. Aurelius PROBUS
282–3	M. Aurelius CARUS

283–4	M. Aurelius Numerius Numerianus (NUMERIAN)
283–5	M. Aurelius CARINUS
284–305	G. Aurelius Valerius Diocletianus (DIOCLETIAN)

The Tetrarchy

West

286–305	M. Aurelius Valerius MAXIMIANUS
305–6	Flavius Valerius CONSTANTIUS
306–12	M. Aurelius Valerius MAXENTIUS *usurper in Rome*
307–37	Flavius Valerius Constantinus (CONSTANTINE I)

East

284–305	DIOCLETIAN
305–11	C. GALERIUS Valerius Maximianus
308–24	C. Valerius Licinianus LICINIUS

The House of Constantine

307–37 CONSTANTINE I "The Great" *sole emperor from 324*

337–40 Flavius Claudius Constantinus (CONSTANTINE II)	337–50 Flavius Julius CONSTANS	337–61 Flavius Julius CONSTANTIUS (II)

350–53 Flavius Magnus MAGNENTIUS
usurper in the West

360–3 Flavius Claudius Julianus (JULIAN "The Apostate")

*

363–4 Flavius Jovianus (JOVIAN)

The House of Valentinian

West

364–75	Flavius Valentinianus (VALENTINIAN I)
375–83	Flavius Gratianus (GRATIAN)
383–88	MAGNUS MAXIMUS *usurper*
388-92	Valentinianus (VALENTINIAN II)
392–94	EUGENIUS *usurper*

East

364–78	Flavius VALENS
379-95	Flavius THEODOSIUS (I)

The House of Theodosius

3795–95 THEODOSIUS I *sole emperor 394–5*

395–423	HONORIUS	395–402	ARCADIUS
		402–50	THEODOSIUS II

*

423–5	JOHANNES		
424–55	Placidius Valentinanus (VALENTINIAN III)	450–57	MARCIAN
455	Petronius MAXIMUS		
455–6	AVITUS		
457–61	Julius Maiorianus (MAJORIAN)	457–74	LEO
461–5	Libius SEVERUS		
467–72	Procopius ANTHEMIUS		
472	Anicius OLYBRIUS		
473–4	GLYCERIUS		
474–5	JULIUS NEPOS	474–91	ZENO
475–6	Romulus Augustus (AUGUSTULUS)		
		491–518	ANASTASIUS
		518–527	JUSTIN I
		527–65	JUSTINIAN I

Further Reading

ANCIENT WRITERS

Ammianus Marcellinus, *The Later Roman Empire*, tr. Andrew Wallace-Hadrill, Penguin 1986.

Caesar, *The Civil War,* tr. J.F. Mitchell, Penguin 1976.

Caesar, *The Conquest of Gaul,* tr. F.A. Handford, rev. Jane F. Gardner, Penguin 1982.

Eusebius, *The History of the Church*, tr. G.A. Williamson, rev. A. Louth, Penguin 1989.

Josephus, *The Jewish War*, tr. G.A. Williamson, Penguin 1970.

Lives of the Later Caesars (The First Part of the Augustan History, with newly composed Lives of Nerva and Trajan), tr. A. Birley, Penguin 1976.

Livy, *The Early History of Rome,* tr. Aubrey de Selincourt, Penguin 1971.

Livy, *Rome and Italy*, tr. & annot. Betty Radice, Penguin 1982.

Livy, *Rome and the Mediterranean*, tr. H. Bettenson, Penguin 1976.

Livy, *The War with Hannibal,*. tr. Aubrey de Selincourt, Penguin 1988.

Polybius, *The Rise of the Roman Empire*, tr. from the Greek by Ian Scott-Kilvert, Penguin 1979.

Suetonius *The Twelve Caesars*, tr. R. Graves, rev. M. Grant, Penguin, 1989.

Tacitus, *On Britain and Germany*, tr. H. Mattingly, Penguin 1948.

Tacitus, *Histories*, tr. K. Wellesley, Penguin 1990.

Tacitus, *The Annals of Imperial Rome*, tr. Michael Grant 1971.

MODERN SOURCES
The following is a selective list, concentrating on recent works which should be readily available to the general reader.

Cary, M., & Scullard, H.H., *A History of Rome,* (3rd ed.), Macmillan 1979.

Cameron, A., *The Later Roman Empire*, Fontana 1993.

Cornell, T., & Matthews, J., *Atlas of the Roman World*, Phaidon 1982.

Crawford, M., *The Roman Republic*, Fontana 1978.

Finley, M. (ed.), *Atlas of Classical Archaeology*, Chatto & Windus 1977.

Garzetti, A., *From Tiberius to the Antonines*, Methuen 1974.

Keay, S.J., *Roman Spain*, British Museum Publications 1988.

Le Bohec, Y., *The Imperial Roman Army*, Batsford 1994.

Randsborg, K., *The First Millennium AD in Europe and the Mediterranean*, Cambridge University Press 1991.

Raven, S., *Rome in Africa* (3rd ed.), Routledge 1993.

Richardson, L., *A New Topographical Dictionary of Ancient Rome*, Johns Hopkins University Press 1992.

Salway, P., *The Oxford Illustrated History of Roman Britain*, Oxford University Press 1993.

Scarre, C., *Chronicle of the Roman Emperors*, Thames & Hudson 1995.

Scullard, H.H., *From the Gracchi to Nero: A History of Rome 133 BC to AD 68* (5th ed.), Routledge 1982.

Talbert, R.J.A. (ed.), *Atlas of Classical History*, Croom Helm 1985.

Toynbee, J.C., *Death and Burial in the Roman World*, Thames & Hudson 1971.

Ward-Perkins, J.B., *Roman Imperial Architecture*, Penguin 1981.

Wells, C., *The Roman Empire* (2nd ed.), Fontana 1992.

Index

Acknowledgements

Picture Credits

Alinari, Florence: 21tr, 22bl, 67, 90
Ancient Art and Architecture Collection, Middlesex: 109, 123
Bridgeman Art Library, London: 57tl, 89
British Museum: 50tl, 54b, 55, 80tl, 96br, 125, 130
Bildarchive Foto Marburg: 57bl
Codex Photographic Archive, London: 14, 18, 19, 20, 24, 28, 37cr, 37cl, 40, 52tl (photos: Ian Johnson), 54cl, 54c, 56, 72, 75, 79tl, 79tr, 79bl, 94, 95, 96tl, 97, 103bl, 108, 111, 117, 119, 120bl, 126, 128bl, 128tl
Deutsches Archaeologisches Institut, Rome: 16bl, 60cr
C.M. Dixon, Canterbury: 39, 78t, 83tr, 92, 104, 118tl, 120tr, 134, 135
Werner Forman Archive, London: 16tr, 17, 21cl (Museo Capitoline, Rome), 37bl, 38, 65, 91, 102 (Museo Nazionale Romano, Rome), 103t (National Museum, Damascus), 106, 115 (Academia de la Historia, Madrid), 129bl (Museo Gregoriana Profano)
Giraudon, Paris: 43
Robert Harding Picture Library, London: 107
Hirmer Fotoarchive, Munich: 127
Michael Holford Collection, Essex: 85, 121
Israel Government Tourist Office: 58
Mansell Collection, London: 34, 35, 46, 52b, 59, 69b, 103br, 131tl
Museo Arquelogico Nacional, Madrid: 12tl
Museo Nuovo nel Palazzo dei Conservatori, Rome: 15
Princeton University (Department of Art and Archaeology) 74t, 77tl
Roger-Viollet, Paris: 62bl
Scala, Florence: 22t, 41, 71, 98, 122, 131tr
Chris Scarre: 12br, 13tl, 25, 26, 34b, 42, 44, 45, 48cl, 60tl, 63, 66, 68, 69t, 74bl, 76, 77br, 80b, 99, 101br, 105, 113, 116, 118b, 129cr, 133tr
Society of Antiquaries, London: 50br
Ted Spiegel, South Salem, New York: 62tl (courtesy of West Point Military Academy)
Vindolanda Trust, Hexham: 78b
Walters Art Library: 37br

Quotations

The author and publishers gratefully acknowledge the following translations from ancient writers used in this atlas:

p.20: Cicero, *Republic*, tr. in N. Lewis and M. Reinhold, *Roman Civilization*, Columbia University Press 1990; p.32: Cicero, *Letter from Rome*, p.34: tr. in Lewis and Reinhold; Vellius Paterculus, *Compendium of Roman History*, tr. in Lewis and Reinhold; pp. 46 & 48: Suetonius, *Lives of the Caesars*, tr. J.C. Rolfe, Loeb Classical Library 1914; p.50: Tacitus, *Agricola*, tr Sir W. Peterson, Loeb Classical Library 1969; p.54: Juvenal,

Sixteen Satires, tr. Peter Green, Penguin 1967; p.58: Tacitus, *The Histories*, tr. Kenneth Wellesley, Penguin 1964; p.72: *The Scriptores Historiae Augustae*, tr. David Magie, Loeb Classical Library, 1922–32; p.78: *The Letters of the Younger Pliny*, tr. Betty Radice, Penguin 1963; p. 82: Seneca, *Moral Essays*, tr. J. W. Basore, Loeb Classical Library 1928–35; p. 99: *Cassius Dio*, Roman History, tr. E. Cary, Loeb Classical Library 1914–27; p.102: Juvenal, *Sixteen Satires*, tr. Peter Green, Penguin 1967; p.104, Pomponius Mela on Africa, tr. in Reinhold and Lewis; p.112: *The Scriptores Historiae Augustae*, ibid.; p.124: Eusebius, *Ecclesiastical History*, tr. G.A. Williamson, rev. A. Lowth, Penguin 1989; p.132: St Augustine, *The City of God*, tr. H. Bettenson, Penguin 1984.

FOR SWANSTON PUBLISHING LIMITED

Concept:	Peter Smith
Malcolm Swanston	Malcolm Swanston
Editorial:	**Index:**
Chris Schüler	Jean Cox
Rhonda Carrier	Barry Haslam
Design and Illustration:	**Typesetting:**
Ralph Orme	Jeanne Radford
	Maggie Slack
Additional Illustrations:	
Julian Baker	**Picture Research:**
Peter Massey	Chris Schüler
Peter Smith	Charlotte Taylor
Cartography:	**Production:**
Andrea Fairbrass	Barry Haslam
Peter Gamble	
Elsa Gibert	**Separations:**
Elizabeth Hudson	Quay Graphics,
David McCutcheon	Nottingham.
Kevin Panton	